HOME IS THE SAILOR,
HOME FROM THE SEA

For Mary Kathreni
Sail around the world
with my father
Ursula McCaffety

To order additional copies, please contact us.
BookSurge, LLC
www.booksurge.com
1-866-308-6235
orders@booksurge.com

URSULA
McCAFFERTY

HOME IS THE SAILOR,
HOME FROM THE SEA

2006

CONTENTS

LIST OF PHOTOGRAPHS

ACKNOWLEDGMENTS

I owe so many people thanks. The first three names that come to mind are Beth Bruno who first got me interested in writing and is now my editor; Jerry Labriola who gave me the push I needed when he told me that I had to write another book; and Liz O'Neil who has given me advice and moral support.

But there are so many more—my cousins in Germany and Africa, Ilo Peeck and Almut Heddenhausen—without them I wouldn't have had my father's letters; Klaus Fuest of the German Shipping Museum in Bremen, Robyn vanDyk of the Australian War memorial, Tido Holtkamp who helped with some of the tougher translations, Donald Hatch who loaned me an excellent German/English dictionary and, last but not least, all the good members of Connecticut Authors & Publishers Association (CAPA) who offer so much encouragement to aspiring authors. A very special thanks to my wonderful agent Debra Fishpaw for her yeoman work and to Dan Uitti, life saver extraordinaire.

Dedicated to my Father
Captain Erich Richter
He sleeps in a quiet graveyard in
the Berkshire foothills of Connecticut
far from his beloved sea.

INTRODUCTION

Erich Richter, born in Germany, followed the sea his entire life. It meant long separations from home and family, but he could never deny its pull. Erich's younger brother, Albrecht, followed Erich's footsteps, while his older brother Robert went on to University and became a Lutheran minister like their father. There is little information available about Albrecht, but Erich wrote volumes in his letters home. He began his amazing adventures when he was not quite sixteen years old beginning as a deckhand on a sailing ship. He eventually went to navigation school and became a licensed Master Mariner. While at navigation school he met the girl with violet blue eyes, Kate Lichtenberg, my mother and the love of his life.

During World War II, I learned of my father's bravery under fire and I knew some of his earlier history as a German prisoner-of-war in Australia. I always felt that I needed to put his life on paper and began with just memories. Quite unexpectedly, I obtained copies of letters he had written to his parents when he first went to sea, the earliest of which were written in 1898. In translating the letters from German to English, I was overwhelmed by all that he had experienced. His first ocean voyage took him around the world and almost cost him his life. In 1903 he wrote about a trip around Cape Horn en route to Chile— a sail that should have been accomplished in two and a half days but was held fast by violent winds and tides for seven long weeks. Quotes from these fascinating letters are sprinkled throughout Part I. WWI broke out in June of 1914 when Erich was a Chief Mate on a German freighter. In October of that year, his ship was captured by the British and he spent the balance of that war in a prisoner of war camp in Australia.

At the close of the war Germany's merchant fleet was handed over to the Allies for war reparations and, after several discouraging years, Erich moved his family to America. There were worrisome times when he was not able to follow his chosen career because he was not an American citizen. As an alien he was unable to obtain his license as a Master Mariner. He finally managed to stay in the United States for five uninterrupted years and qualify for citizenship and his certification. During those five years he worked at many different jobs from barge captain on the Hudson River to pier superintendent in Brooklyn.

During WWII Erich was a Commander in the United States Merchant Marine. He dodged submarines in the Atlantic Ocean and ice in the Barents Sea.

His entire life was filled with close encounters with danger. He was not so fortunate in the Mediterranean where his ship, carrying a volatile cargo destined for Salerno, was torpedoed by a German submarine. His actions under fire were credited with saving a very valuable war cargo and for that he was honored with the Merchant Marine Meritorious Service Medal.

***

Many months into the writing process I discovered that my mother had started to write my father's biography in 1933. She had written on loose sheets of paper in German and in a small notebook in English. Her notes helped fill in many details for me. Her introductory page was entitled "My Dear Husband, Erich Richter" followed by the statement: "His life from deckhand to Captain. There were many happy and some sad years, but he was always brave despite many reversals. Dedicated by his Kate."

Part One

THE EARLY YEARS

Chapter 1
The Deckhand

Even real heroes have humble beginnings and my father was no exception. His youth was filled with adventure and hardship. Indeed, throughout his life he chose the road less traveled.

Gustav Adolph Erich was born in the village of Panzfelde, Germany, August 14, 1882. He never used the first two names and was always known as Erich. He was one of eight children born to Pastor Robert Richter and his wife Olga. Three boys, Robert, Erich, and Albrecht, and one daughter Else, survived to adulthood. Their father had accepted a parish in Sundhausen, and it was from there that Erich's adventures began.

They were typical rough and tumble "preacher's kids." The boys were full of mischief and their mother was the disciplinarian. She was small of stature but had a mighty will. When the boys got too rambunctious, she picked up the nearest thing she could find and swung. On one such occasion, Erich was her target and her weapon happened to be a stick with a nail in it, which scratched Erich. He howled and told her that she had damaged his left lung. His mother's caustic comment was, "Turn around and I will damage the other lung." Obviously this was a time before children were given "timeouts" in a room full of toys and a television set. Punishment was harsh and immediate. The one girl in this clan, Else, became something of a tomboy in sheer desperation.

Pastor Richter was not just a preacher; he was also a teacher. The children were educated at home by their father and were schooled in the classics and mathematics. The natural progression from home schooling was to prep school That meant conforming; it meant no more running wild in the village; it meant no more fun, and above all, it meant separation from family and all the assorted pets and livestock. For a wild and free country boy this was not an easy transition. Erich arrived at his new school in the town of Nordhausen when he was just 15 years old, dressed in a suit his mother had made for him. The suit was a horrid shade of tan, which inspired some of Erich's new classmates to become creative in the insults they hurled at him. But Erich, as one of three boys, had learned to hold his own and promptly settled the matter with his fists. He decided that this "sissy" school was not for him; he wanted adventure. How a boy from the Hartz Mountains, far inland from the sea, had developed such an urge to become a sailor is something of a mystery but that was what he longed to do.

***

His father, a mild man and a scholar, was somewhat disappointed that Erich's energy was not directed towards furthering his formal education. Perhaps Erich's desire for a more active rather than passive life style was inherited from his grandfather, a Prussian army Major. Erich's father reluctantly gave permission for Erich to leave school. The stipulation was that he could not change his mind in a few months and again opt for school. He was obliged to make a choice, and he chose the sea.

He went to Bremerhaven, the port of Bremen, and applied for work as a deckhand on any sailing ship that would take him. He was hired as a hand for a four-mast barque named the *Dorothea*. The *Dorothea* was classed as a full-rigged 4-mast, deep water, sailing ship. Her specifications were as follows: length 62.2 meters (68 yards), breadth 10.1 meters (11 yards), draught 8.3 meters (9 yards), tonnage 1033 gross tons. She was originally launched in 1870 and was then, in April of 1898, in dry dock in Norway for maintenance.

After I read these specifications I paced off 11 yards in my small apartment. The thought of 15 men living in such narrow quarters for months on end, through wind and rain and violent storms, staggered my imagination.

Erich was sent to the harbor to board a ship for Christiania (Oslo) Norway; from there to be transported overland to the *Dorothea*. The smell of the salt water was like a magnet to him. The activity around the port, the ships, sailors, even the seagulls wheeling above, were part of the magic. He was going to fulfill his dream. He could not have wished for more. He, along with the ship's carpenter, the cook and the chief mate, boarded the *Kon Ranan* on Friday, April 15, 1898, at ten in the morning, bound for Christiania. The steamer finally sailed in the afternoon and evidently they had received nothing to eat. For a teenage boy this was agony, and he bemoaned the fact. *"The steamer didn't sail until four o'clock and we had to starve until nine. The dining area was below decks... our pigsty at home is better."*

On Friday evening Erich got seasick, but was quick to assure his family that he was only sick *"for about five minutes, not longer."* It's surprising that he even owned up to a momentary weakness, but throughout his letters, he seemed to feel it necessary to be totally candid and honest with his family.

On Saturday he experienced his first storm at sea which he described as: *"One wave trying to swallow the next one. The ship first climbed high in the air, almost like riding up in a balloon, then down again, with water pouring over the railings."*

On Sunday they arrived in Christiania after crossing the beautiful Christiania Fjord. They were to stay on board until Monday, then go to Station Sandefjord, the drydock where the *Dorothea* was undergoing maintenance. Erich and the cook and carpenter all managed to go ashore and he describes the town as *"very pretty with many marble houses."*

They had just returned to the ship when they received a change of orders. They were to leave for Station Sandefjord, by train, that night. After unloading crates and sacks, they were driven to the train station at seven. The train was not due to leave until midnight. Again he mentions food. *"We hadn't eaten in nine hours so we went into a hotel and each ate an English beefsteak. It was tough as horsehide."*

At the end of a four-hour train trip, they arrived in Sandefjord and, finally, at 11 o'clock, he stepped aboard the vessel that would be his home for many months. It was April 20, 1898.

The Alsterfee, identical to the Dorothea
From the archives of the "Deutsches Schiffahtsmuseum (German Shipping Museum) Bremerhaven, Germany

Erich was immediately put to work on a large winch on deck where he worked with a sailor until one o'clock in the afternoon. Then he was called to help the cook prepare the meal, which consisted of pea soup with carrots, salted potatoes and salted meat and, he still didn't get anything to eat. Then he was back at the winch until four p.m. At four they received chicory water (which was probably a substitute for coffee), hard tack and butter. Each person was allotted one pound of butter per week.

While in drydock, the *Dorothea* had been reinforced with iron bracings. At four-thirty that afternoon, it was time to bring her out of the drydock. This was evidently not an easy job since Erich refers to it as *"a job I don't even want to talk about."*

They finally finished at ten in the evening. They were scheduled to sail for Friederichsstadt at one-thirty, but were delayed by bad weather. He commented, *"Thank God it was stormy so we couldn't put to sea...the ballast was too small and had shifted."*

They returned to the cabin until five-thirty a.m. when they were called out again. At six a.m., they were back to work down in the hold that was full of water. They had to carry the ballast, consisting of stones weighing upwards of 50 pounds, to the hatch area. At eight, it was time to get breakfast...boiled rice with syrup over it. They then winched up the anchor and set the sails. The tug *Odin* brought them close to Friederichsstadt. There they dumped their ballast and also encountered a fierce snowstorm. April is not a warm month in northern Europe or in Scandinavia. Snowstorms are not uncommon even in New England in April.

Just reading about the first few days of Erich's new life makes me wonder how some of today's fifteen-year-olds would react to such a regimen. Of course our child labor laws would never allow it to happen.

The *Dorothea* was expected to stay in Friederichsstadt no more than 14 days, and Erich urged his family to write to him right away so that their letters would reach him before the ship sailed. For all his boyish bravado, it was apparent that he missed his family and friends, and yet he was happy in his new life despite having to work so hard. There appeared to be a shortage of hands because five sailors had deserted on the first night, and although three were returned to the ship, they again deserted the following night.

The master of the *Dorothea* was Captain Fischer, who seemed to be kindly disposed to Erich. Most of the crew was Swedish and Erich was the only inexperienced hand on board. The other deckhand was from Berlin, and Erich describes him as, "*19 years old, already five years at sea and still a deckhand,*" a clear indication that Erich intended to do better.

The rules for progression up the ladder from deckhand were as follows: a man could sail as an able-bodied seaman if he had three years sailing experience as deckhand and ordinary seaman. With just one year as deckhand, two and one half years as ordinary seaman were required. If, on the other hand, a man had two years as deckhand he need only sail one more as an ordinary seaman to attain the rank of able-bodied seaman.

In Friederichsstadt, the *Dorothea* took on a cargo of oak boards. Oak boards were Friederichsstadt's only export, and each load was bound for Australia, the opposite side of the earth. Even today, Australia is half a world away from the northeastern United States and requires eighteen hours of airtime to reach it. What an endless expanse of ocean lay between these men and their destination!

The cargo was not the only thing to arrive on board. A new deckhand was added to the crew. This one hailed from "Elsfleth" (my mother's home town). He, obviously, was not too bright. Erich describes him as follows: *'The new colleague's name is Karl. He has what the first mate calls 'shellfish eyes.' When he is supposed to bring wood, he drops it on the chief mate's head, or he addresses the captain as 'du.'* [1] *He has already received several lashings."*

The fact that Erich accepts the idea of "lashings" as a legitimate way to maintain discipline indicates just how common a practice this was. The daily routine for the hands involved getting up at four in the morning and washing down the decks and frequently working "topside."

They were required to haul the water in order to scrub the decks down, often slipping and falling on the wet decks, causing bumps and bruises, and in some cases, even broken bones.

On May 1, the weather in Norway was still quite cold. In a letter home, Erich requested some wool, some patches, an old jacket and his pocketknife. The sailors had lent him an old jacket because he couldn't wear his good one and all the rest of his gear was summer clothing. By May 15th his package from home had already arrived. Although Germany and Norway are not that far apart, I was surprised to read that his request of May 1st had already been honored by the 15th. He wrote a thank you to his parents and announced that he would have to move the buttons on the jacket since it had become too tight for him. In spite of a less than perfect diet, he was evidently going through a typical teenage growth spurt.

The next letter is from Sydney, Australia, 133 days later, dated September 25, and Erich described the journey in detail. His home schooling had taught him how to write an intelligent and informative letter. The ship had sailed from Norway on the morning of Ascension Thursday, May 19, 1898, and arrived in Sydney on September 23. The long journey was filled with new experiences for a boy from a land-locked town in the mountains.

The weather in the North Sea was fine, but in the English Channel they encountered fog and thunderstorms.

Erich got his first opportunity at the rudder and quickly learned to steer...a heady experience. Once on the open Atlantic, he saw his first porpoise, which he described as, *"a mammal with snout and teeth."* The chief mate harpooned a fat one weighing about 400 pounds. The two- inch layer of fat was stripped off and boiled down to make oil. He describes the meat as *"delicious, looking something like horse meat but tasting like the finest duck drumstick."*

The following night his watch on deck was from midnight to 4 a.m. He was on outlook from 12 until 1, and from 1 to 2 at the rudder. Suddenly the second mate stepped up to him and asked if he had heard something. Erich told him that he had been concentrating on watching the compass. The mate then told him to listen very carefully. Soon he heard a strange distant sound he could not identify but it kept getting louder. *"Suddenly the moon rose and cast a silver light across the water. It was now 2 a.m. and my turn at the rudder was over. I was relieved and took a watch position still trying to identify the sound. All at once a huge creature rose, not 10 meters from the vessel, and spouted a great stream of water. But that was only the beginning. Shortly we were surrounded by a herd of approximately 50 whales. The sight was awesome."*

This would still be an awesome experience today, even for the most jaded. How much more so for a country boy!

On July 3 at 10:30 they crossed the equator and the traditional baptism of "first crossers" [2] was held. The carpenter, an ordinary seaman, and Erich were the ones to be baptized by "Father Neptune." The sailors grabbed them by the collar when they tried to hide. One after the other they were soaped and shaved with a two- meter long blade. *"I can't even begin to tell you all that was in that 'soap' but I recognized coal tar, oven rust, fish oil, black soap, green paint and a good dose of the contents of the officers latrine. Three times we each received a mouthful of that delightful 'soap.'"*

If this didn't sicken them it, should have made them immune to almost anything they might encounter.

The ship then sailed along the coast of Africa. As they neared the Cape of Good Hope, the wind turned and the weather got colder and became decidedly unfriendly. They were crossing at 50 degrees south, the same latitude as the Falkland Islands. With atlas in hand, I tried to trace the entire route and decided that I would not undertake such a journey on anything less that a modern cruise ship.

The weather was such that they all wore two heavy woolen shirts, two heavy sets of undergarments, two pairs of socks, boots, a woolen vest and a watch jacket. Still, if they hadn't donned their oilskins on top of all that, they could not have withstood the cold. Furthermore they were in danger of collision with the icebergs they saw looming around them like great landmasses.

About 3 or 4 degrees south of Tasmania, (approximately 47 degrees south) Erich tells of seeing the amazing Southern Lights for several nights. *"But they were not a good omen, because we ran into a fierce storm during which our first mate was lost."* In a few days they sighted Sydney. They hoisted their flags and could have been in port in four hours but suddenly the sails filled and they were turned away from Sydney. Erich stated that this was their salvation because that evening they weathered a severe Australian thunderstorm. I'm not sure why they were safer out at sea than in port during a thunderstorm. I contacted the University in Melbourne, Australia, but never really received an answer to that question. Perhaps there was a greater danger of being dashed on rocks inside the harbor.

In all of his letters Erich confirms his faith in God. He closed the first letter from Sydney assuring his parents that he had not forgotten the "Our Father," and that he prayed each night for those near and dear to him to be kept safe. Erich ended all of his letters with love for his family and greetings

11

to friends and relatives and signed each one, *"your loyal son and brother, E."*

He said that he was well and happy and that he had grown a foot taller and was the second tallest on board. As far as lashings were concerned, he commented that he had received his share in the beginning but that it didn't matter …he could laugh at it now. Erich assured his parents that he was content and that his career suited him. He was looking forward to spending some time in Sydney and then going on to Newcastle, Australia. From there the ship would probably go to the west coast of South America.

On October 27, he wrote from Newcastle. Erich described Sydney as very nice and since he was expecting to stay longer, he had planned to write again from there. He was unable to do so because, as usual, they had little advance notice of when they would be leaving. Eighty-five more cords of wood were unloaded in Newcastle, and the journey, now, would take them to the west coast of Mexico to Acapulco with a load of coal. Erich commented, *"When I finally come home I will have been around the world in one trip! I have learned that, with God's help, all things are possible."*

He wished his family a Merry Christmas and regretted not being able to stand in the candle glow of the Christmas tree with them but assured them that his heart was with them. He also requested that they send him a few photographs and told them that it would be a while before they heard from him again. They were heading for New Zealand and the South Sea Islands. *"But console yourselves with the words of one of our seaman's songs, 'God leads the sailor home through storm and danger.' God be with you, he will reunite us in good health and happiness."*

On November 14 another letter from Newcastle describes the preceding days: *"In Newcastle we off loaded the last of our cargo. Then we went to Stockton and from Stockton back to Newcastle and moored at the coal dock. In two hours we loaded 600 tons of coal. The railroad cars were hoisted over the main hatch and their load tipped right into the hold. Now we are dumping the ballast we loaded in Norway."*

He goes on to say that in both Newcastle and Stockton he had often been ashore doing errands for the officers. He was quite proud of his ability to bargain and said it was a good way to learn English, but he was looking forward to going back to sea because they were *"tormented by mosquitoes, fleas, and rats."*

The harbor in Newcastle must have been a bustling place. Erich tells of seeing ships from many nations. Although today's young people are far more likely to have traveled and seen something of the world, what an amazing experience for a boy of 16 in 1898! And now he was embarking on the journey across the mighty Pacific Ocean. The expanse of the South Pacific and the Pacific Ocean between Australia and the west coast of Mexico is tremendous. Although no mention is made in any of Erich's letters about stopping at any of the South Sea Islands I can't help but wonder if they stopped for provisions or water. It would have been a shame to miss the beauty of those exotic South Sea Islands.

Erich thought that after Acapulco they might go to Punta Qxnar in Costa Rica and, hopefully, from there to Bremen, possibly by October 1899. Little did he realize what still lay ahead of them.

On March 19, 1899, the first letter home after Australia, came from Acapulco. Erich was thanking his parents for the wonderful package he had received containing pants, stockings, handkerchiefs, sewing material and some photographs. But what made him happiest was to hear that all his family was well. The *Dorothea* had left Newcastle on December 1,1898, and headed south passing New Zealand and the Auckland Islands. At Christmas there was evidently much celebrating because he describes it as *"just a lot of whiskey and grog."* But in his heart, he was at home with family. He again refers to the candlelit Christmas tree and the beloved Christmas songs. Even in later years, I remember how he loved to sing and how special Christmas was to him.

On the second day of Christmas, they encountered a strong hurricane that created violent seas. *"It was so violent that a large English ship had 16 men washed over-board...all 16 drowned. Our total crew is only 15."* After the storm they had nice weather and reached Acapulco in ten days. Erich's description of Acapulco as it was in the spring of 1899 is a far cry from the tourist Mecca that Acapulco is today. *"I have not yet been ashore but I can tell you it is a pitiful place...nothing but straw and mud huts. The heat is awful; you cannot walk barefoot on deck. All the natives carry large daggers in their belts. The only other ship here is a Norwegian barque. She left Friederichsstadt three hours after we did and went to Port Elizabeth. We met again in Africa and now we meet yet again."* This was the first reference to any stops having been made in Africa and no port is mentioned.

The ship was expected to stay in Acapulco for approximately two months, then go on to Punta Anna for orders before heading home to Hamburg or Bremen. *"I probably will not be home before next Easter. The trip from the west coast (South America) can be made in about 3½ months, but often takes 7-8 months."* It is difficult to envision that any destination on earth could take that long, when, today, we can fly from the United States to Europe in hours.

On April 16, Erich tells of having been bitten, in the lower leg by a mosquito. From his description it is difficult to believe that an ordinary mosquito could have inflicted so much damage. The bite became very painful. In his sleep, he scratched the bite and the next morning his entire leg was swollen and blue. The captain sent ashore for a doctor, who, after prescribing various salves and ointments to no avail, planned to operate the next day. The doctor had barely left the ship when Erich applied one of his mother's homemade plasters. *"The very next day a two inch break appeared,"* he wrote. *"Blood and water poured out. Two days later I was back on deck."*

The crew was busy loading sand ballast into the main hatch; 300 tons would be required before sailing. It was planned to discharge cargo within the week and be ready to sail in about 14 days for Punta Arenas.

Erich refers to news in a letter from home regarding the death of a neighbor. *"The last time we shook hands he said to me, 'Who knows if we will meet again, out there you could drown.' And I answered him, "Well, on shore a rock could fall on your head."* There is no reference to the cause of the neighbor's death, just to the irony of fate.

May 25th, the *Dorothea* was in Punta Arenas, Costa Rica, and Erich had received letters from home. He was disturbed that none of his earlier letters had reached his family. Orders had just arrived for the ship and Erich surmised that the orders would be for Puerto Cohbra, Costa Rica. *"But don't picture it as a city, because our anchorage will be in a jungle...just one building. Therefore you must address your letters to Punta Arenas, where they will lie until we return. The loading of lumber is tricky and will take about 2½ months. You won't hear from me for quite awhile, but you are not to worry. We are in God's hands."*

On July 8, 1899, a letter from Puerto Chobra finds Erich well and happy. The ship had been hauled ashore in Punta Arenas, and the hull scraped before proceeding to Puerto Chobra. Their cargo consisted of huge cedar logs. *"Below decks is pretty full, but now it will go slower because a Norwegian and an English barque are also loading here now. In spite of the unbearable heat, it is really beautiful here; we are in the middle of a jungle. It abounds with monkeys and parrots. We tried to catch one but didn't succeed. There are also many other creatures here. There are sharks in the water and snakes on land. This place was named for the latter. One morning at six, as we started to work, a Swedish sailor and I went to open the rear hatch. We hadn't finished unlatching it when the sailor ran away. I thought he had forgotten something and wanted me to do the job alone. I was suddenly startled to see a three-foot long snake coiling itself at my feet. I didn't have much time to think. I still had the iron key ring in my hand. One slash, fortunately, was enough to kill the reptile. It was a very poisonous snake.*

We will be loading for another 1½ months; then we will return to Punta Arenas for orders. We will probably be paid off in Hamburg or Bremen so there is no point in sending me anything, although your good will is appreciated. Besides, nothing would reach me now. By the time your package would arrive in Punta Arenas we would be well out on the high seas."

He related the snake incident with such candor and then went right on to another subject. I wonder if he was trying to sound nonchalant to his family. He must have been pretty frightened when he suddenly was faced with a three- foot long snake.

August 27, 1899, from Punta Arenas, Erich writes that he was expecting to put to sea the following day, destination either Hamburg or Bremen. He relayed the Puerto Chobra experience as follows: *"We were in Porto di Chobra (difference in spelling is my father's) for 12 weeks loading cedar wood. During that time the second mate took ill. Since there was no doctor to be found, he opted for a 200 mile trek through the jungle to Punta Arenas for help. After much searching, a native was found who was willing to guide him. He had to travel by dugout to Platz Sardenal. It was a terrible blow to hear, three weeks later, that the second mate had died. He was a young man of only 24 and died because of contact with a dirty woman."* (Erich's words!)

I wonder who taught him all about venereal diseases and their dangers? I can't picture his mild father, the pastor, imparting such knowledge to a 15 year old. And his mother, though tough lady that she was, can hardly have been expected to hold such discussions with her sons.

Erich's narrative continues: *"When the ship was loaded we returned to Punta Arenas, thank God, the last foreign port. But we still have the long journey ahead of us around Cape Horn and the English*

Channel, where there is lots of cold and wind. The wind is the best part as long as it does not come from in front of us. This will be the last letter you receive from me from a great distance. The next word from me should be in person: about the end of February."

He closes this letter, *"God grant us a joyful reunion."*

***

"The plans of mice and men go oft astray"
Robert Burns.

***

There is no written record of the following 175 days. The joyful reunion at the end of February did not take place, because, by February 21, 1900, Erich was near death in a hospital in Ponta Delgada, the Azores. Why it took the *Dorothea* almost six months to travel from Chile to the Azores must remain a mystery. The probability is that the trip around Cape Horn, dicey at best, may have seriously delayed them. Late summer is also Atlantic hurricane season and a hurricane could well have been a contributing factor. Whatever the reason, the 175 days at sea took their toll. In that length of time their food supply could have been greatly diminished except for, possibly, fresh fish. The South Atlantic is practically devoid of the type of archipelagos found in the South Pacific.

The passage from South Atlantic to North Atlantic runs right through "hurricane alley." So there were certainly many possible scenarios. The two worst enemies of old time sailing ships, beriberi and scurvy, established a firm foothold on board.

On February 28, 1900, Erich wrote the following letter:

Dear parents and siblings,

Thank God with me for His rescuing me from grave danger. If we had been at sea any longer I do not think I would have lived three more days. Allow me to describe for you the agonizing pain.. the scurvy is terrible. My legs are crooked and stiff; below the knees they are gray and black. The flesh on my arms is loosened from the bone and so I have great pain while writing this letter. My gums are black and bleeding and have a terrible odor. On February 18, an ordinary seaman died at sea. He was sewn into canvas and consigned to the sea. Fortunately we arrived here on February 21. The night of the 21st, Captain Fischer died. When the doctor arrived on board he established that the two worst illnesses with which seamen can be afflicted, beriberi and scurvy, were both present on board. Eight of us had scurvy, two had beriberi, one died of scurvy and Captain Fischer died of beriberi. The only healthy ones were the chief mate and the cook, but two sailors were also allowed to stay on board. We, the remaining eight, were taken ashore and to the hospital on stretchers. Hundreds of people had gathered to look at us. By the time I reached the hospital I was near death. But God in heaven be thanked, from day to day we are improving. Although I feel otherwise well, I still cannot stand on my legs for even a minute. I do hope to fully recover in five to six weeks. If the ship isn't here that long, the German consul will have to transport us to Hamburg. Then I will come to visit! A German sailor, a stranger to us, came to visit us in the hospital. He gave me an envelope and a stamp so I got out of bed and crawled on all fours to the table to write this. I consider it my duty to keep you informed. Soon you will hear more from me, but now my arm is very painful.

***

Since beriberi and scurvy are hardly commonplace today, I researched the two illnesses to better understand what these men had suffered. The following is from the American Medical Association Home Medical Encyclopedia:

***

Beriberi- a metabolic disorder from lack of vitamin B (thiamine).

Symptoms: Two forms of illness – "dry" and "wet" beriberi are recognized. In "dry" beriberi, the thiamine deficiency mainly affects the nerves and skeletal muscles. Symptoms include numbness, a burning sensation in the legs, and wasting of muscles.

In severe cases, the patient becomes emaciated, virtually paralyzed and bedridden.

In "wet" beriberi, the main problem is heart failure (inability of the heart to keep up with the task of pumping blood). This in turn leads to congestion of blood in the veins, and edema (swelling caused by fluid collection) in the legs and sometimes the trunk and face. Other symptoms include poor appetite, rapid pulse, and breathlessness. As the heart failure worsens, breathing becomes more difficult and, without medical treatment, the patient will die. Treatment consists of thiamine given orally or by injection, which brings a rapid and complete cure.

Scurvy: A disease caused by inadequate intake of Vitamin C.

Inadequate supplies of Vitamin C disturb the body's normal production of collagen (connective tissue). Collagen continues to be produced but it is unstable causing weakness of small blood vessels, and poor healing of wounds. Hemorrhages may occur anywhere in the body. They are most obvious in the skin, where they result in widespread bruising. Bleeding from the gums and loosening of the teeth are common; bleeding into the muscles and joints also occurs in scurvy, causing pain.

When scurvy is treated with large doses of vitamin C, bleeding stops in 24 hours. Healing resumes, and muscle and bone pain dissipate.

***

How frightening this whole experience must have been for the men on board the *Dorothea*. Certainly the experienced seamen must have realized how dangerous their situation had become and how desperate they must have been to make landfall---any landfall. The Azores were evidently not a planned destination, but a heaven-sent oasis to a dying crew.

Erich returned home and was placed under a doctor's care. His illness weakened his heart muscles and his recuperation took time. His father offered him the opportunity to go back to school but he chose the sea.

***

Pastor & Mrs. Robert Richter—Erich's Parents

Chapter 2
The Ordinary Seaman

In June of 1900, Erich had recuperated enough to, again, follow his heart to the beloved sea. On June 21, he mustered on as ordinary seaman on the barque *British Princess*. He had planned to muster on a ship named *Industrie* but couldn't wait to earn a living. The *Industrie* would not be ready for sea for several more weeks and no crew would be hired until the ship was ready for sea. The captain of the *British Princess* was Captain Kohler, a man with an excellent reputation. Erich signed on at 36 Mark, six Mark more than the other ordinary seamen because he had already sailed for 18 months. He describes the ship and itinerary as follows: *"The ship is a large barque of 1400 tons and is in Scotland. On Monday 17 of us will leave, by steamer, for Scotland. Some of the crewmen are already on board. The trip goes to New York and from there, with petroleum, to Yokohama and then to the saltpeter coast.* [3]*"*

On June 26th Erich arrived in Leith, Scotland on the British steamer *Breslau*. The complement on board the *British Princess* totaled nineteen, not counting the captain's wife and children. It was not uncommon for wives and children of the ship's officers to accompany them on long journeys. Erich assured his parents that he was feeling well and looking forward to the upcoming trip.

On June 29th his assessment of the *British Princess* had altered slightly. *"The British Princess isn't worth much, but she is supposed to be excellent under sail. The captain is a very good man and we are confident about the future. The chief mate also seems to be a good person so far. The second mate was also an outstanding man, and it would have been so nice, but God help us, it was not to be. This morning the three ordinary seamen, an able-bodied seaman and the second mate were at work between decks where we found a ton of sand, Just as we were about to throw it out, 10 rats ran out and immediately attached themselves to our pant legs. Only the second mate was spared. He tried to pull back quickly from the attacking rats, but he lost his grip and his footing. A single yell, a dull thud and all was silent. At first we were too stunned to move but then the able-bodied seaman climbed up on deck and we ordinary seamen climbed down into the lower confines of the ship, which only held ballast. The second mate had fallen approximately 20 feet and had landed between rocks (used for ballast) the size of tables. He lay unconscious, blood pouring around our feet. When the captain and the chief mate and several sailors came, we lifted him carefully into the light. Our combined efforts succeeded in restoring him to consciousness. But how? His whole head was battered, both arms broken and probably internal injuries too. It was terrible to hear him groaning so. The ambulance arrived in ten minutes. I will visit him on Sunday. With God's help I hope he will recover."*

On July 3, the ship was officially renamed from *British Princess* to *Luise* and Erich writes, *"Life on the Luise leaves nothing to be desired."* The second mate was doing much better than they had thought possible. In fact, he was already back on board but not yet back at work. The itinerary now read a little differently. *"The day after tomorrow we will leave early for New York. There we will load petroleum for Yokohama and from there we will go to a port near San Francisco to load lumber for Europe. It will probably be just around Christmas when I return. I am well and happy."*

After 45 days the *Luise* arrived safely in New York, and now Erich was faced with the possibility of a 180-day trip to Yokohama. Having just recovered from scurvy, and obviously still feeling some side affects, Erich expresses doubts about making the long journey. *"Although I can see the trip to Japan could take 180 days, I am inclined not to go along. Not to run away, mind you, but to be properly paid off. I have spoken to the captain about it and he agreed with me. Don't worry that I am sick or anything, but just for safety sake, I will be examined by a doctor. If there is anything wrong, I will go to the hospital at the ship's expense. Then I can, either return there via a Lloyd steamer and sail along the*

German coast, or for the time being, sail along the American coast. I will see."

He also makes reference to things not looking good in China, evidently due to the "Boxer Rebellion."

After his usual greetings to family and friends he added the following PS: *"Do not worry about the first part of this letter, because no one can blame me if I don't feel that I can go on such a long trip."*

On September 3, he reports on the outcome of the visit to the doctor, which resulted in a five-day stay in the hospital. Since he received no medication, one must assume that the hospital stay was for observation only. The captain of the *Luise* managed to secure another position for Erich on a ship named *Birma*. This entailed going back to Germany and immediately mustering on a steamer bound for New York.

He expected to leave within the week. Upon arrival in New York he Wrote: *"New York is a giant city. Right in the harbor the Statue of Liberty reaches out her hand and there is a huge suspension bridge [4], and Coney Island."*

On October 1, 1900 Erich is in Altona, a port area around Hamburg. His well-laid plans are, again, altered by fate. He left New York on the steamer *Burgermeister Petersen* and would have been happy to return to New York aboard the same ship. Unfortunately the ship was first going to dry dock in England. This would have delayed Erich too long to connect with the *Birma*. There was not enough time to muster on to another steamer and still make the connection, so he considered trying for a small sailing vessel to the West Indies.

He describes his trip from New York as somewhat hair-raising. *"On September 11 I went on board and we sailed immediately. Had terrible weather. We had barely cleared the American coast when we ran into a West Indian hurricane that killed 7000 people and wiped out entire towns in Texas and cost $15 million in damages. The storm drove us with violent force. The coast of*

Newfoundland was already visible and we expected to be driven ashore momentarily when the wind shifted and drove us eastward. The weather did not improve throughout the trip. After a nineteen-day journey we finally arrived at Swinemunde. I would have loved to come home but I don't have the money to do so."

He goes on to say that his references from the *Luise* rate him as "very good" except one for behavior which was listed as "praiseworthy."

The hurricane to which Erich referred was the great hurricane of September 1-2, 1900, which raised havoc and caused major death and destruction in Galveston, Texas. The *Monthly Weather Review* of September 1900 listed 6000 people killed and damages as high as 30 million dollars. It was the tail of this killer storm that nearly drove the steamer *Burgermeister Petersen* aground on the coast of Newfoundland.

By mid October, Erich sounded almost desperate in his search for work. He told his family that there were a lot of people in Hamburg looking for work. He had been offered a position on a small sailing ship plying the North Sea. He was uncertain about accepting. He tells them he would let them know. His very next sentence was, *"Leaving on a fish cutter in 15 minutes,"* and he asks that letters be addressed to him in Altona.

On October 30 Erich had returned to port on the *Landrat Kuster.* He told his parents that he was well and alert and discussed how difficult it was to obtain work in Hamburg. It was because of the scarcity of jobs that he had decided to accept the job on the fishing vessel. Evidently, in spite of good food and good treatment, the situation was less than idyllic. Erich had been hired as an ordinary seaman and had been obliged to cook, which made him angry enough to break several pots. I guess patience was not one of his virtues, at least not in his youth. The pay was less than satisfactory. He had earned just enough to pay the board bill run up in Hamburg before he set sail. It was his intention to make only one more trip, lasting about 14 days, and then try to muster on a steamer.

At the age of 18, Erich had seen and experienced so much, and yet he tells of another sea tragedy.

***

"At the mouth of the Elbe River, we witnessed a sad ship tragedy. It was stormy with high seas. From the Weser River lightship we were sailing with a large Bremer four-mast ship with a load of saltpeter from Caleta Buena, near Iquique. A tugboat approached with an offer of a tow but the captain thought the price too steep. At the third Elbe lightship the vessel turned to take a pilot on board. Unfortunately the vessel began to drift and beached on the strand. The waves poured over the deck and the masts broke. The ship began to sink. The Elbe lightship sent out a lifeboat which capsized, its crew of three men hanging on and being washed out to sea. No one knows what became of them. With that, the beached vessel launched lifeboats, of which one capsized. At this point, 12 men had been lost. If the captain had accepted the offer of the tug, this would never have happened."

***

November 12th finds Erich back in Altona where he was being relieved of duty. He commented that he would be hard pressed to find another vessel where the food is as good as on the *Landrat Kuster*. *"I am well and now weigh 144 pounds! When I was home I weighed 133. This has been a bad year for fishermen. In the past they could earn 400-500 Mark on each trip. Now they barley make 200 Mark. I learned a great deal which will be useful to me as a chief mate. I would gladly have sailed with Hinrich Wolf if the winter in the North Sea didn't hold me back. There is nothing to be gained out there but a severe case of rheumatism."*

Again his ambition shows through in his reference to what will be useful when he is a chief mate.

On November 16, a brief letter home states,

"Thank God, I now have a job as an able-bodied seaman on the schooner Tuterina under Captain Onken. I am only earning 40 Mark a month but, with times as bad as they are, one has to be thankful to find any work. The ship is going to England. I don't know anything further as yet. All is well, going aboard immediately."

Chapter 3
Good Ship, Bad Ship

A new phase had begun for Erich. He had progressed from deckhand to ordinary seaman and now to able-bodied seaman in two years. He was just 18.

December 9, 1900 finds him in Poole, a seaport on the south coast of England.

"We are here with five men on board: the captain, who is also the owner (27 years old!), a chief mate, another able-bodied seaman, an ordinary seaman and a deckhand who is also the cook. We had loaded linseed cake as we left Hamburg. Because we could not sail on the Elbe one afternoon, we anchored and therefore had to furl the sails. The other able-bodied seaman and the ordinary seaman were on one side of the yardarm and I was on the other side. I went to the outer edge to fasten the sail. Suddenly I heard a loud cracking sound and I called to my colleagues, 'I think the yardarm is breaking!' 'Oh, where?' called William. I went further but held on. I had gone but two steps when what I feared actually happened. With a terrible crash the yardarm broke right where I was standing. Just by leaping away, very quickly, I was spared a broken neck. I only sprained my hand. God certainly was holding his hand over me...all honor to Him."

The William referred to was an 18-year-old orphan Erich had met in Hamburg. William's father had been a carpenter on the Lloyd steamer *Elbe* and was drowned when the ship sank. William's mother had died soon after. Erich described his meeting with William as follows:

"On November 16 we were both at the employment office where we were almost crushed to death and still didn't find work. On the way, we met Huerbass (another sailor) who had a job. He said if we had come earlier, we both could have gotten a job on the same ship. William, my

colleague, rode along to Harburg and I went home (evidently to his boarding-house room.). In the afternoon I was hired for the steamer Belgia. I went for a physical and as I was leaving, one of the men made a slanderous remark about the 'run-away preacher's son.' I immediately demanded my muster book be returned, and told him off. He quickly backpedaled. (Erich's short fuse was very evident when it came to slurs on his character.) When I arrived home my friend was delighted to tell me that we could both get on the same ship. I am only earning 40 Marks but it is better than earning 60 as a steamship lackey. The Tuterina is a good ship and the food is good. In spite of my best intentions, I am unable to send you more than the 9 Marks. If I have anything left over, I will send more"

I gather that Erich tried to send money home to his family whenever possible. Whether that was to repay a loan or just out of duty, I do not know.

On December 14th the *Tuterina* was still in Poole. The captain was in the hospital awaiting throat surgery. The broken yardarm had been replaced with a new one. Since his whereabouts at Christmas were still not certain, he wished his family a joyous holiday.

On December 25, he wrote a thank you to his parents for their invitation. *"Your loving invitation we accept gladly and are already looking forward to the shining Christmas tree."*

Evidently his parents had invited William to come home with Erich for a post Christmas visit.

The captain's surgery was another blessing in disguise. Had they left Poole when first planned, they might not have survived. Erich explains,

"The schooner Frederike left Harburg (a section of Hamburg) at the same time as we did and in Poole we were side by side. The two captains are from the same town, even neighbors. The Frederike left Poole eight days ago. As the ship was leaving the harbor her captain called over to us, 'When I have brought my ship to Plymouth I will come

back to get you.' The following week it was very stormy and we were unable to leave. On Saturday, when the weather improved, we set our sails and were already in Plymouth on Sunday. Today is Tuesday and the Frederike still has not arrived. Even the captain's illness was the hand of God, for if he had not been ill we would have sailed with the Frederike. Then we too would be lost with our brave comrades. "Last night, on Christmas Eve, we had a lot to do. In the evening the captain sent us two packets of cocoa, a can of salmon and fresh bread. This morning we received a can of sardines, a can of milk, two more packets of cocoa and fresh bread. This afternoon I read the scripture reading for the day and we prayed the 'Our Father.' We are loading clay and will go directly to Harburg. There we will first have to unload the ship and clean it. This should take until the middle of January. Then we will leave our gear in Harburg and come home to celebrate Christmas with you in the light of the glowing Christmas tree. We are already filled with joyful anticipation. When we come home we would like to receive Communion."

I can't help but wonder how severe a fire hazard a three-week-old, candle-lit Christmas tree would have been.

***

January 6, 1901, finds Erich's hopes dashed again. The late Christmas reunion with his family was not likely to be. The loading of clay, a type used in the manufacture of porcelain, was complete. The wind was coming from the east and useless for a sailing ship heading eastward. He told his parents, *"I will write again from Harburg. If a trip home is at all possible, even if only for three days, we will come."*

It is evident that holidays were not necessarily a "day off" for the crew.

"New Years day we had to really work hard... it was necessary work. Today (Jan 6), Epiphany Sunday, the captain sent the chief mate out to tell us to wash the deck down. I told the mate we were not

servants. The mate, who is a good and pious man, relayed the message to the captain. The captain came tearing out to give us a good dressing down. He babbled so long that I jumped out of the cabin and threw my boot against the door. This startled the captain so that he fell backwards and landed on the part of his back we don't like to discuss. He hurried back to his cabin and didn't show his face again until tonight at 12:45. We stood up and sang 'A Mighty Fortress is Our God' and several other hymns, after which I read the Epistle for Sunday. Saturday we had to work until two in the afternoon. When the entire cargo was loaded, lunch was prepared. Not ten minutes later, the Englishmen demanded that the chief mate call us out to bring the loading chutes ashore. At that point, my colleague William was dueling with an Englishman who was swinging a 20 pound piece of clay. He boldly went into the battle and the Englishman fled bleeding."

Erich declares that he is feeling better but has heard sad news. *"I heard that a steamer from Bremen, Luise, was lost all hands on a trip from New York to Yokohama. I don't know if it's true but I hope it isn't so."*

The *Luise* was the ship on which he sailed to New York in August of 1900. The captain's wife and children had been aboard. Erich seems to have been either very lucky or very blessed with his life careening from one   narrow escape to another. Throughout his lifetime, fate seemed to have stepped into the breach and steered him away from disaster.

On January 17, 1901, he still writes from Plymouth, *"We are at anchor here because of high winds and also the Elbe River is still full of ice. I probably will not come home because it will be too late and my clothing isn't decent enough. I will have to buy a suit and shoes. The chief mate told me how I can get a 'made to order' suit for 33 Mark. I don't know if I will get that much money."*

His letter was a little disjointed because he was surrounded by a lot of conversation, but he did say that he hoped to leave for another trip at once, if possible. He thought he might be able to earn 50 Mark on the next trip.

By March 22, Erich had mustered off the *Tuterina* and was preparing to board a mail steamer named the *Hamburg*. The ship was scheduled to leave on April 2 for Gibraltar, Suez, Port Said, Colombo, Singapore and Yokohama. The trip was to take four months. After a brief visit to the *Hamburg* Erich describes her as a twin screw, fast steamer.

The captain was Captain Krech and the crew consisted of 16 able-bodied seamen, 6 ordinary seamen, and Chinese deck hands. They were only hiring experienced sailors, and Erich was expecting to be paid 30 Mark.

Life was certainly never dull for Erich---at times uncomfortable and at times dangerous but never dull. His first letter home from the steamer *Hamburg* is a perfect example:

"On the Hamburg we are a total of 20 able-bodied seamen; but sadly there are 50 Chinese stokers aboard and the whole foredeck stinks. Yesterday evening I was in their quarters and there I saw what they were really like--- the smell was terrible. There were at least ten sticks of opium being smoked. (The smell of opium was evidently a new and unpleasant experience for him and he made his distaste for the smell as well as for its affect on the users very plain.)

"Over there was one that looked dead, another had fallen asleep while smoking. In the corner on a chest they had made an altar and there were bits of silver and gold paper burning on it." (To a staunch Lutheran this strange worship appeared to be a pagan ritual; we have come a long way in our acceptance of other cultures since 1900.)

"Today they attacked the three German head stokers. They trapped them in a narrow passage and attacked, with knives, hatchets and bottles. Because the passage was so narrow we couldn't get in to help. We connected hoses and let the pumps run full power. We soaked

them so thoroughly that they let their victims escape. Fortunately none of the three head stokers were seriously injured."

His attitude regarding the Chinese stokers came from a total lack of experience with the Asian cultures. In later years Erich learned a great deal and shed the bigotry born of ignorance.

Erich promised to buy a tea service for 12 when he got to Yokohama, and as usual, sent his love to all his siblings. He seemed to be somewhat perturbed about his brother Albrecht, when he wrote, *"I want to please you and Albrecht. But I will then demand that Albrecht comes home, then goes together with me."*

In many of his writings home, Erich inquired about Albrecht. Albrecht had also decided to follow the sea and Erich appears to have been anxious to meet up with him and, perhaps, travel with him as shipmates. At no point can I find a record of Albrecht actually connecting with Erich, nor of Albrecht making a great effort to visit home. He became something of a ne'er–do–well, drinking and womanizing, the proverbial "black sheep." Brother Robert went off to University, studied theology, and was ordained a Lutheran minister. Erich chose a different path but honor was always his guide. How one of the three brothers could have gone so wrong is a mystery.

April 1 was the last evening in port for the *Hamburg*. German stokers were hired to replace the Chinese stokers. The "battle of the stokers," was evidently covered by the press because Erich asks his parents if they had seen anything in the papers about the fighting.

The next correspondence from the *Hamburg* is hardly a glowing report. It was written on April 14, just before arrival in Genoa.

"We arrived in Antwerp on Good Friday. The passengers were awakened by the band playing, 'Jesus My Savior.' We, on the other hand, had to work like beasts until we were drenched in sweat. On the first day of Easter we left Antwerp and, again, had to labor the entire day. On the second day of Easter we arrived in Southampton, where we spent the entire day loading gold and silver chests. In the evening we sailed. We were barely out to sea when we ran into a pretty strong storm. The 'Gentlemen Officers' were so clever that they steered the ship, at full steam, into the storm for 15 miles. It didn't matter to them; only the sailors were getting wet. They were safe and dry up on the command bridge while we were up to our necks in water. Suddenly a large wave washed over the ship. We all held on as well as we could but the wave caught the largest and strongest of the seamen and tossed him, with tremendous force, between three emergency anchors that were lashed on deck. When we reached him his whole head was battered and his right ear was missing. He had a severe concussion but if he hadn't been wearing his southwester [5] *he never would have moved again. "We don't just have to work all day but also at night. The watch that comes on deck at 8 p.m. starts washing at 10. When the next watch comes on at midnight, they immediately begin washing until 4 a.m. until the first watch is back and begins working again. So it goes, night and day, weekdays, Saturdays, Sundays...never a moment to gather your wits. When I get to Bremerhaven I will immediately go to Cenbrock and Blank* (evidently a hiring agency) *and leave my muster book there and come home, only to bring the things home."* (The "things" to which he refers are evidently the souvenirs and tea services he planned to buy in Yokohama.)

Erich's religious convictions were offended by the fact that the crew was compelled to work without respite on such holy days as Easter, with no time set aside for prayer. He made his feelings clear with the following statement: *"My Christian faith does not allow me to stay aboard this ship. Dear parents I don't know what you think of this. If this letter disturbs you I am truly sorry but I only told the honest truth. Here on board they don't even want to give me a postage stamp for my letter since I have no cash. But now I must close…the work begins again."*

On April 19, 1901 the *Hamburg* was about to make port in Port Said, having stopped in both Genoa and Naples. There were several hundred passengers aboard, including several officers with troops ordered to China. Captain Krech had been promoted to inspector and had gone ashore in Genoa. The new captain's name was Makin. Colombo was the next port of call and in his letter, Erich expected to arrive in Colombo on May 3. He appeared to be counting the days until his commitment to this vessel was over. He asked his family to send him stamps so that he could mail his letters to them since the paymaster refused to part with a cent. It appears that, while at sea, there was no salary paid out, just rations. The wages were evidently paid out at the end of the trip when the crew mustered out. This put the crew almost in the "slave" category. What option did they have but to stay on board until the ship returned to Germany? These were not the days of strong unions and protests.

May 2 the *Hamburg* was approaching Colombo and was expected to arrive at six the following morning.

"Maybe there will be a letter from you waiting for me. In Aden we lay at anchor. We arrived at ten in the evening and left at five the next morning. Today is the sixth day out from Aden. From Suez on it was very hot and I witnessed one case of heat stroke. I, myself, am quite well and hope that you are the same. Last night there was a large masquerade ball aboard which, of course, meant that we had a lot of extra work.

"The two and one half months will pass. On July 23, according to plan, we should be coming to Bremerhaven, but there are always a few days discrepancies. Last Sunday was our first free day since coming aboard. I put on a clean shirt every day now since cleanliness is half of living. One perspires so much! Yesterday we met a four mast barque that had lost her masts."

May 12th they had already made a 24 hour stop in Singapore and were en route to Hong Kong where the plague was running rampant. They were to stay one day and then go on to Shanghai where Erich was looking forward to finding mail from home.

He again expressed his disappointment with the situation on board.

"Here, on board, it is the same old complaint—work night and day, and the food isn't great either. I am now on room watch whenever we are loading or unloading cargo; this is only since Singapore when two strangers were chased away. It is a responsible position and one must work day and night, but it is still quite an honor. I can hardly believe they have chosen me for this since I am the youngest of the eighteen sailors. Altogether there are five sailors on room watch, each to watch over a separate hold, to assure that the loading is orderly, nothing is stolen and nothing unwanted added. The last few days it has been very hot, but today it was a little cooler. There have been cases of heat stroke, malaise, and falls. One steward died. He had fallen about midday and the doctor, a real greenhorn, declared him a malingerer, and he was forced back to work until he fell over dead. This is how it goes on the famous passenger ships. The officers play the part of "big shots" and would like nothing better than to have us as slaves. Our first officer is the biggest..? (word illegible) *at sea. He just wants to put us down. Recently we were asked to sign something. When it came my turn I said I would have to read it before I could sign. This made him angry and he called me a bull. I answered, 'Oh, I have always been one.' That made him even madder, as though I had argued with him for an hour. My record is still very good. There are three men on record for drunkenness (one month labor.)"* That was his last letter from the Hamburg.

URSULA McCAFFERTY

Chapter 4
Trading Ships

Erich survived the trip and, on August 18, he was back in Bremerhaven aboard the *Atlantic,* which he describes as an old ship with poor rigging. *"We could not ask for better food."* The ship was bound for New York. The trip was estimated to take about 60 days. They actually made the trip in 56 days.

"We had a lot of stormy weather and that is really something for an old wreck like the Atlantic.

I want to draw a picture for you but I must start back at Geestemunde (part of the port of Bremerhaven.) Saturday night at 3 o'clock we sailed out of the harbor and Sunday, on the river, we loaded powder, dynamite and ammunition. After that we went to sea. As far as food and drink is concerned, this is the best ship so far---but the equipment— --every 2 hours we have to pump and everything is fouled up and rotting. The Atlantic is a special ship for anyone to gain experience. In the sailors' quarters we are seven able-bodied seamen, two ordinary seamen and fourteen hands. I have formed a strong friendship with another sailor named Luis Salvor from Wiesbaden. We want to come home together to then go on a long trip with Albrecht. Albrecht has surely come home safely by now. I would love to be able to travel with Albrecht once if he can wait for me. It wouldn't hurt him to wait. Our destination has not yet been decided. If we take on cargo here, we will probably go to France or England; but should we go to Savannah then our destination will probably be Rotterdam or Hamburg. But it really doesn't matter...even if the trip costs 100 Marks I will come home if Albrecht will wait for me."

Erich's disappointment continued. In October he again expressed surprise that Albrecht didn't even drop him a few lines while he was at home. He included a special note addressed to Albrecht:

Dear Albrecht,

If you want to wait until I get there we can make a trip together. I will bring home another sailor, there will then be four acquaintances in one crew. That can make quite a difference. You undoubtedly know your own job and anything you do not know will be easier to learn from your brother than from a stranger, and I know my job. I don't mean to boast, but I can be honest with my brother, especially if we want to travel together for a year or two. Therefore, I urge you to reply to me and let me know what you think. With greetings and brotherly love I remain your loyal brother,
E.R."

***

Erich was, evidently, quite fond of his brother and disappointed that Albrecht seemed to make no effort to join him. Perhaps Albrecht didn't want his brother looking over his shoulder and dampening his enthusiasm for the seamier side of life. We never talked about Albrecht very much, but I remember my mother saying that she felt sorry for his "poor wife."

On November 11, 1901, Erich's letter home congratulates his parents on their silver wedding anniversary and wishes the family a joyous Christmas. He mentions having received a letter from Albrecht and is disturbed about his brother's plans. Albrecht had evidently turned in his muster book and was planning to go to Canada to work on the Great Lakes.

"You can only earn a few cents and have to work cargo night and day, which does more harm than good. It is much better to make long trips on ships out of Bremen---the best of sea life. I wasn't born yesterday and I will say in advance that Albrecht will bitterly regret

going to Canada. I will not go under any circumstances and neither will my friend Luis who has been in Canada. This is a bad idea and I seriously discourage Albrecht from doing this. We can talk about this when I come home. Eight days before Christmas you can write to me at Rouen and let me know if he has received his muster book."

Erich had described the *Atlantik* as an old wreck of a ship and by November 29th he was no longer a member of her crew. He had transferred to a ship called the *Landseer* out of Bremen.

"I will explain how I happened to have left the Atlantik. November 20th was a day of penance. We were supposed to work but declined which angered the "old man" so that he wrote us all up in the Journal. Then two of us went to the consulate and the captain was forced to let us muster off. We had to leave 60 Mark for a replacement crew but we gladly did so. We were ashore just three days, living in private accommodations, and succeeded in finding work on our own. We will earn 70 Mark a month until we reach London. Don't let Albrecht leave and have him make sure his papers are in order. Then, if I stay on the Landseer, he can join us in London. Maybe I will stay on to give Albrecht a chance. I think we will be in London in 30 days, so write soon as I think we sail tomorrow. On the Atlantik the 'old Man' took on five new sailors and the next morning only two were left. The Landseer is also a wooden ship but ten times better than the Atlantik.

On January 2, 1902, Erich was back in England.

"We arrived safely on December 31 after a 26 day crossing, despite severe North Atlantic storms. (The ship must have picked up westerly winds to make such a rapid crossing.) I am not sure whether or not I will come home. I may go to Hamburg or Bremen if I can't get another German ship here. Although the Landseer and Captain Henes are very good, I don't feel like staying aboard because of the dangerous cargo she carries. Anyone lighting a match is fined 100 Mark; no lamps may be lit. During the day we work and at night we aren't even able to

write home. I am writing this in a tavern. We are docked here, 30 miles from London, in the middle of a wilderness."

In the early 1900s the communities at the mouth of the Thames River, such as Gravesend, were more sparsely populated than in the current time. Docking areas for ships were rarely right in the town but rather on the outskirts.

"On Christmas we had very bad weather. On the first day of Christmas, we Germans had a little devotional service whereupon one of the Swedish sailors laughed and said, 'When you're sick it's time enough to pray.' I answered him, 'No one knows when death will greet you.' On the second day of Christmas we were wakened at 8 a.m. As we came on deck, we saw that our ship was surrounded by a whole school of porpoises. We immediately got harpoons and headed for the bow to catch fresh fish. Suddenly a huge wave came and washed the Swede overboard. We were under storm sail and the ship was running at eight miles an hour so it was nothing short of a miracle that we had the man back on board within two minutes. He thinks differently about prayer now."

Recently, I obtained a notebook in which Erich had written a lot of his poetry. Included were two stories, one entitled "Man Overboard" which is a more graphic account of the preceding incident; it follows herewith:

MAN OVERBOARD
By Erich Richter

Personal experience aboard the full rigged vessel Landseer, Christmas,1901 in the North Atlantic Ocean

Christmas Eve--- it is wild. The storm is howling and roiling the ocean so that the sea is pounding mountains of waves against the hull of the old wooden ship. At times it seems as though the ship will never reemerge from under the awesome load of water that pours over her decks. Only storm sails remain and the wind is howling through the usually peaceful rigging. As wild as it is outside, here in the sailors' quarters we are celebrating Christmas. The sailors of the free watch are gathered around an artificial tree created from a broom and painted green. They represent many nationalities. Next to the Germans are the sons of Norway, Sweden, France and Holland; but all are thinking of loved ones at home and singing songs in their native tongues. The room is doubly bright with the glow of the Christmas tree. The captain has brewed a strong punch so happiness and joy reigns despite the ferocious storm outside. And so it continues until, on deck, a bell sounds announcing that we must relieve the watch in 10 minutes. The ship is on its way from New York to London. We are in the grip of a westerly Storm that has plagued us since we left New York and rapidly carried us towards the English Channel. Tonight the weather is no better. The hard-working vessel is already taking on a lot of water, but in spite of the reefed sails, the pump windmill is being continually driven so there is no cause for worry. Another morning and nothing is better, but suddenly the ship's dog begins barking loudly to announce that dolphins are near the ship. Everyone rushes to get the harpoons. Charli Hedmann, the big Swede, grabs a harpoon and jumps on the bowsprit while the rest of the watch mans the rope to haul in the catch. We can almost taste fresh fried fish. Suddenly the ship climbs skyward and, just as quickly, plunges down into the boiling sea. We all hang on for dear life-- even Charli. He takes the greatest pressure because he is only standing on a pair of chains and is dunked, knee-deep, into the sea. But *the sea is not done with him; once more the ship rears up and plunges down and this time he is immersed to his armpits. The harpoon slips from his hands and he is torn from his slippery perch into the violent sea. In the first moment everyone was stunned but almost immediately the cry rings out, "Man overboard." But who can help? The second mate is still back at the jib-boom, the Captain and the Chief Mate are in the cabin eating breakfast and the off-duty watch is in the lounge. The cook is the first one to recognize the alarm. He rushes forward to find a line to throw overboard—something for the unfortunate man to cling to--but to no avail since everything is tightly lashed down to prevent the violent waves from washing anything overboard. The off-duty watch, arriving on deck to help, is immediately tumbled around by waves washing over the deck. They have all they can do to keep themselves from washing overboard. The Captain and Chief Mate were still in the aft cabin enjoying a leisurely breakfast. The howling wind outside does not let the alarm penetrate to the rear cabin. At that very moment the cabin boy came on deck, also unaware of what is happening. The cook yells at the cabin boy, "Throw the 'Grossbrass'* [6] overboard." The cabin boy immediately throws the line overboard, almost without thinking. Now too, the first sailors arrive on deck and see their comrade wallowing in the sea. By all calculations, he should be far behind the ship that is moving at about eight miles an hour. However he is a born swimmer and spends no time worrying about his fate. The ship turns and he quickly grasps the bracing beneath the forward sail. But immediately the ship pushes him so far underwater that he loses his grip. 'Now,' he thinks 'all is lost,' when suddenly the line thrown by the cabin boy sails past his ear. He grabs hold, but as the line goes taut, due to the ship's movement, he almost loses his grip again but fate smiles on him. Every hawser has a heavy knot at the end so that it will not slide completely through the block & tackle and be lost; it is this knot that makes his rescue possible. When the line was thrown it tangled around one of the ship's rails and the knot caused it to tighten. As the line tightened, Charli had the good fortune to be able to lift a loop over his head and so he is roughly towed behind the ship. But it doesn't last long; twenty hands haul the trembling man on board. Both the Captain and the officers are* *now on the spot and the Captain, a giant of a man, examines Charli for broken bones. The only damage is a black eye. Recently Charli had sustained a black eye in an encounter with 'Blackadder,' but this time it was truly different. When he first lost his grip on the bracing, he banged his head against the side of the ship and, not only, got a black eye but almost lost consciousness. Only through his colossal energy and willpower was he able to keep his wits. He certainly must have told himself, 'If I get behind the ship it will be too late...in this sea it will be impossible to launch a boat.' The only damage, other than the black eye, was the loss of his rubber boots that the strong sea had pulled off his feet while he was dragged back to the ship. A strong cognac restores him and one hour later Charli is back at the helm steering the Landseer towards the English coast. He becomes a little thoughtful and comments, 'Next year I will have to make certain not to be in the North Atlantic on Christmas.'"*

***

It became apparent that Erich also thought "differently" about the *Landseer* and her dangerous cargo because on January 11th he wrote from London, *"I am thinking of staying on board since I have never had it so good and will probably never have it this good again as on the Landseer.* (He had changed his mind about going home.) *What's the point of coming home now and being broke. If I wait until July I will have 300 Marks saved. Still, could you, if possible, send me a little package with a watch and tobacco? That would be fine, but maybe also a shirt and some socks and some German sausage would be wonderful. Could you send it soon?* (Erich, at the ripe old age of 19, still seems to long for treasures from home.) *We are leaving in about eight days. We do not know our destination yet---maybe the West Indies. As soon as we reach Nordfleth, (Northfleet) I will write more detail. I have to close now but I beg you to reply soon, since I have waited ten days to hear from you."*

Erich had reached the age to fulfill his military obligation. On January 16, he requests his father to obtain a one-year deferment for him.

"In regard to the military, I have asked Captain Henes to straighten it out with the Consul, which he has promised to do. But it is better, dear Papa, if you can get me a years deferment and forward the same to New York.

I think we will sail tomorrow at noon. We loaded the rest of our ballast today. The entire crew is staying on board; isn't that a good sign? I am healthy and alert, the food is outstanding, and one could not wish for a better captain and officers."

The crossing to New York took 60 days. When the ship left Northfleet it encountered a Channel storm and they were obliged to ride at anchor for 12 days. They sailed southward, through snow and ice, to reach the warmer southern waters and the trade winds. The trade winds blow westward towards the earth's equator in both the northern and southern hemispheres. They occur approximately between latitude 30 degrees north and 30 degrees south of the equator. The name *trade winds* comes from an old sailing term that meant the winds could be counted on to blow steadily from the same direction at a constant speed. This took them well away from the bitter North Atlantic winter.

When they were south of the West Indies they turned northward and let the warm southerly winds drive them at the rate of 12 miles an hour. They were hoping to reach New York the following day but the weather changed.

"Suddenly a storm, from the north to west, brought snow and ice. The change was terrible. It's a wonder all of our bones didn't freeze. The weather held for 14 days until we entered New York harbor. Yesterday I received your dear letters and the package and thank you for all. I was happy to hear that you are all well as am I. I have an excellent ship. Everything on board is very good. This morning we each received two baked eggs with ham and also two colored Easter eggs for breakfast.

We got so much cake we couldn't even finish it. We don't know yet where we are going, maybe France. Thank you for all you sent me, it was very good."

April 8, 1902 Erich is still in New York and having second thoughts. He is finding it difficult to save money because one dollar is equal to 4.25 Mark and *"spends just like a Mark."* In effect, everything was four times dearer in New York than in Germany. He was also a little uneasy about the dangerous cargo of naphtha. Erich began formulating his plans for the future. *"I may stay on board for one more trip, come home for Christmas and then make one more long trip. I'm thinking, with God's help, to go to Bremen about April 1, 1904 to navigation school. What do you think about that? Write soon."* In actuality, Erich attended Navigation School in October of 1904.

His appearance must have changed considerably from the time he had been in New York aboard the *Atlantik*.

"When I was here on the Atlantik, I had one of my pictures painted. It was finished too late for me to get it then, but arrived on board last Saturday. It is exactly like the photograph but none of my comrades want to believe that it is supposed to be from a photograph of me because I have changed so much."

***

Erich at age 19
from a tintype painted in New York in 1901

***

By April 8, the *Landseer* had already been in New York for 14 days and was chartered for London. On April 27th the ship was in Staten Island, New York, and Erich refers to the place as an out of the way place. It is difficult to imagine anywhere within the city limits as being "out of the way," but there is still more open space on Staten Island (Borough of Richmond) than in most of the other New York City boroughs.

They were loading naphtha and alcohol, a highly flammable cargo and Erich declared that, before he would sail on another "naphtha clipper" he would buy life insurance. He was planning to go home about the 20th of June and hoped to meet up with his brother Albrecht.

After a 35 day trip, the *Landseer* arrived in the Thames harbor on June 5.

Erich had received letters from home. There is a touch of bitterness in his reaction to the news that Albrecht didn't wait for him:

"I am just sorry that Albrecht doesn't have a few weeks time to wait for his brother. I was so looking forward to the reunion. But if he doesn't care I can manage without him. I don't know if I will come home. I am definitely going to Hamburg or Bremen in about 14 days. I will then take a ship that will stay away at least 16 months.

On this trip we had good weather, which was lucky, since we might not have been able to bring the Landseer home without it. The ship developed a leak and we had to pump night and day to keep her afloat."

He was to be paid off with 200 Mark once the cargo was unloaded. He comments that all traces of the scurvy are finally gone and he is in good health.

By July 9, 1902, he had already obtained a new position on a ship the *J W,Wendt*. He wrote a letter to his sister telling her that the ship was about to be towed to Shields, England. There was a lot of work to be done on the ship's rigging. On

July 20 they were preparing to sail for Valparaiso, an estimated trip of 100-120 days. He found it quite pleasant on board. *"We have a good cook and the captain too, seems to be very nice. Also the second mate, with whom I am on watch, seems to be very nice. The chief mate is a 'monkey'. The crew consists of young men, a total of 24, and a little cat. We will be back in about ten months."*

The fact that Erich always judged a ship first by its cook is probably due, in part, to the fact that during the final days on the *Dorothea*, before she reached the Azores, food was extremely scarce (close to non-existent.) Erich was also in his greatest growing years from teenager to manhood, and food is always a major consideration to any growing boy.

The trip to Valparaiso seems to have been accomplished in approximately 91 days since, in his letter of November 11, he told his family that the ship had already been in Valparaiso for three weeks and was expected to be there for about five more. Erich appeared to accept small disasters as routine. In discussing an accident, he covered it briefly and then promptly went on to another subject, making the entire letter sound a little disjointed.

"We have to work very hard here. We also had an accident that, fortunately, turned out alright. The handle of a winch hit ordinary seaman Winting from Blumenthal in the head, smashing his skull so that the brain was exposed. Miraculously he is on the mend. I was ashore once and it is very nice here. Next Sunday I will go to the Seaman's Mission. The pastor was on board today and kindly invited us. Recently there was a bad accident on the Norwegian bark Prinz Arthur. The sail maker, while fastening a sail, fell from the large yardarm onto the deck. We summoned a doctor but death had been instantaneous. The brother of the unfortunate man is aboard another Norwegian ship berthed next to the Prinz Arthur. The beer here is very good -- too expensive, but it tastes wonderful. Because the coke [7] is so dusty, we have to flee not to get smothered. We often laugh at ourselves because we look so funny; we are as black as Moors, with white eyes, red

lips and white teeth. All the same, everyone is in good spirits. Evenings we make music and sing. One Swede ran off so we are all Germans in the crew quarters. The Swede was a troublemaker and, one day, he acquired a beautiful pair of black eyes. That's why he ran off--- so much the better. Where we are headed after here we do not yet know. The saltpeter trips are not too bad. I think we will go to Portland or Tacoma. As soon as there is anything positive, I will write."

On December 8 the ship was still in Valparaiso.

"We had a holiday today because the feast of the 'Immaculate Conception' was celebrated. Tomorrow morning at 6 we will be back in the hold shoveling coal. It is pretty hot here. Hopefully, by the beginning of next week we will be finished discharging our cargo. At present there is nothing forthcoming as to freight for the return. We are hoping that the Wendt will get a load of saltpeter [8], in which case we will probably be home in June. However, if we go to North America we will not be home until October."

Erich was content on the *Wendt* because he considered the food particularly good and received enough money to occasionally go ashore. He commented that a very good Pilsner beer was brewed in Valdiera and that there were quite a few Germans living there. He had also heard that one of his former ships, the *Landseer* had been sold in New York due to old age. Ten days later he writes,

"Today I can give you good news. Tomorrow we will have finished with our cargo. On Tuesday we head for Tocopilla to load saltpeter so that we will be clear for sailing home to Hamburg by January 15. We will hopefully be home by May. For Christmas we will be at sea.

Here everything has its ups and downs. Last Sunday we had a bloody scene. The first carpenter was ashore and got so drunk that he wanted to murder us all. He went after one man with a large hammer and a long knife, but his intended victim beat him so severely that he lay

on deck all night and wanted to die. Now he's under doctors care; his eyes are swollen almost shut, his nose and his head are broken, he is limping around on one leg and can't work. I guess he wont try that again."

By January 7, the *Wendt* had arrived safely in Tocopilla, but as usual, plans had changed once more.

"A huge strike has broken out here so we will have to load the saltpeter ourselves, which can take another four weeks. We won't receive our orders until the ship is cleared for sailing. It is much hotter here than in Valparaiso. Tocopilla is a miserable place...no trees, no grass grows here. There hasn't been a drop of rain here in ten years. There are thousands of seals here. Yesterday we saw a shark, over twenty feet long, tear apart an ox."

There is a long gap in the letters from January 7 until June 4. What happened on the *Wendt* will have to remain a mystery.

Chapter 5
Saga of the Nesaia

In June, Erich is aboard the *Nesaia* in North Shields.

"I am looking forward to going to sea because, honestly, I can't wish for anything better than I have now. The cook is good as well as the crew and officers. The day before yesterday, I had a little accident- - I tore my right arm on a rusty nail but ignored it.

The next morning the whole arm was swollen. I went to the captain who quickly lanced the arm which gave immediate relief so that I didn't waste a single hour."

He refers briefly to something that happened on the *Wendt*.

"We will probably go to Puerta Caleta and Iquique to discharge cargo. You will have to write by the end of August and to the address in Taltal so that the same thing doesn't happen as on the J.W.Wendt. All letters will be forwarded."

It sounds as though his mail was either lost or had been tampered with . . .possibly the work of his former friends? This might explain why he had previously expressed disappointment that some of his letters had not reached his family. Lui was the former friend Erich had been planning to take home with him for a Christmas visit to Sundhausen. He must have done something very mean for Erich to make such a turnaround. On June 30 he mentioned meeting Fritz and Lui in Bremen: *"I really told them off. Captain Wolters told Fritz he had never before seen such meanness."* In the same letter Erich describes the *Nesaia:*

"Although the food on the Nesaia is not as good as on the Wendt, there is nothing the crew is lacking. I'm fifth oldest among the crew."

Erich always loved music and delightedly related, *"The music is terrific: 3 flutes, 2 accordions, 5 harmonicas, tambourine, drums, kettledrum, triangle, violin and zither."* He not only loved music but was also quite a poet. There are pages of poetry in his notebook that, sadly, lose something in translation. I do know that, years later, whenever he was home and he and my mother were going out, he would leave me a note--- always in verse, sometimes serious and sometimes whimsical. Unfortunately, when I was a teenager, it never occurred to me to save these treasures..

The following is a letter dated August 2, 1903, San Vincente, Cape Verdi Islands.

Dear parents and siblings:

I hope this letter finds you all well. You will be wondering why you are receiving a letter from here. We turned in here to put our sick captain ashore. We anchored two hours ago. Maybe we will continue tomorrow to Taltal. I am very content on the Nesaia. I hope to God it stays the way it is now; just the food could be better. I am on the second mates watch, he is the best one I have had so far. As we left Shields, we immediately ran into a terrible storm in which we were underwater more than on it. In pitch darkness we missed, by a hair, being rammed by a steamer. It was only by lighting emergency flares that we were spared being sunk. Also, in the Channel, we had bad weather to start. Today, on the twenty-eighth day of our journey we sailed into San Vincente in an emergency. I will write to you once more and let you know if the captain will go with us. Such good officers I have not had for a long time. One really has to admire and respect them. Thus far not a single bad word has passed between officers and crew."

***

But the adventure was just beginning.

On September 6 Erich wrote from Rio de Janeiro describing the trip to that point:

"The captain did not go ashore in San Vincente; instead he went back to sea with us. When we were just a few days out he went stark

raving mad...so bad that we steered right for the coast of Brazil to land at Pernambuco. When we crossed the equator we had the Neptune baptism for the first(equator) crossers. On my birthday (August 14) I was lucky. We had the morning watch from 8-12 in our cabin. As we were eating breakfast, the cook suddenly called that there were porpoises off the bow. We ran out and I was fortunate to hit a large one with the first throw of my harpoon. It took a lot of effort to bring the big fish aboard. We dressed it and had fresh fish every day for three days but then had to toss the rest overboard as it was too warm to keep.

"As we approached Pernambuco, the captain seemed to get better so we steered away from the coast again. We were not very far off shore when the cargo began to heat up and give off gas. The temperature in the hold was up to 48 degrees Celsius (approx 119 F). We expected an explosion any minute. Finally the heat in the hold eased off. The wind turned southerly and it got cooler. We were out to sea from Buenos Aires when the captain started his craziness again, so we turned around to gain the harbor. The captain will probably stay here and the first mate will become the captain. Otherwise everything is fine between officers and crew. Rio de Janeiro is a beautiful city but the fever is raging here.

Just as we were entering the harbor, a corpse floated past."

***

The fever raging in Rio de Janeiro turned out to be the very least of their troubles. In November Erich wrote his next letter home. The exact date was not quite legible but I assume that it was near the beginning of the month since they left Rio in September. After his usual salutation and greetings to his sister and her fiancé on their engagement and a wish that they wait for the wedding until his return, he described the journey since September.

"As you know, we left the captain in Rio. The chief mate became captain and the sail maker became boatswain, As we left Rio we had the finest weather and sailed to Cape Horn in about 10 days. Suddenly

the heat in the cargo hold began to climb and reached a high point of 54 degrees Celsius (131 F). Luckily the Nesaia is the first German sailing vessel to be equipped with a coal gas quenching system. The only question was whether or not the system would work. If it had not worked, no one would ever have heard a word from the Nesaia again. To add to the trouble, it began to blow, mightily, out of the southwest, bringing strong hail. We could not go forward. On October 6, we had a 4-6 hour rest time but were barely in when we were called back on deck to save the sails. We reefed the mainsail and the foresail when suddenly there was a loud crash. I didn't see anything but a terrible rush of blood, pouring from the back onto the foredeck. The ordinary seaman, Albrecht Achenbach from Limburg on the Lahn, had fallen from up top and landed directly on his head. I have seen a lot but I am still overcome when I think of it, how the poor man was lying there in front of us. Blood was pouring out of his mouth, nose and ears, which lasted about 20 minutes. The whole left side of his head was smashed and his brain was protruding out of his ear, and still the unfortunate one lasted another hour and twenty minutes. As we gave him a little wine, he hemorrhaged severely and died. Ever wildly the storm raged and we had to batten down everything and lash all but the mainsail. The waves were huge. We were to help at midnight and I went to the captain and asked if he wanted all our lives on his conscience, but he said if we didn't make it around (Cape Horn) we would have to beach. With God's help we made it. If one of those huge seas had washed over us, the entire crew would have been lost.

On the next day we didn't want to commit our dead comrade to the sea because of the continuing bad weather, but when the bad weather continued into the third day we finally decided to proceed. It fell to my watch to sew the body into canvas. It was a difficult and gruesome job since the body had begun to decay. But finally the job was done and we gathered on the afterdeck at 8 o'clock; the flag was lowered to half-mast.

We couldn't lay by because of the fierce storm. The captain couldn't speak clearly because the tears were flowing into his beard. The chief mate prayed the 'Our Father' and we all took off our southwesters. Never have the words of a clergyman had more impact than the 'Our

Father' on the afterdeck of the Nesaia during that storm which lashed us with a fresh onslaught of snow and hail. In that single week, we were driven back 77 miles instead of going forward. Cape Horn held us captive for 7 weeks, a trip that we could have sailed in 2 ½ days. The entire time we never got out of our oilskins. Hein Bussenschnitt and an ordinary seaman were tossed over the rudder and another sailor from our watch fell on the slippery deck and was knocked unconscious. He recuperated but was laid up for 14 days. With God's help we have finally arrived but are under quarantine because we came from Rio. We have received our order to proceed to Caleta Coloso where we have to discharge 1000 hundred weights of coal (5 tons). With the rest we are to sail to a saltpeter place. It will be the end of May before we will be back."

Erich urged his family to write to Caleta Coloso *"right away"* so he would still receive their letter, and he wishes the family and friends a Merry Christmas and a Happy New Year. He was not looking forward to Caleta Coloso. *"Caleta Coloso is 100 miles north of here, close to Antofagasta. It is supposed to be an awful hole---just two houses and a factory, so no picture post cards from there."*

One of the most frightening periods of Erich's sailing experiences took place in Caleta Coloso, Chile. The build-up of coal gas in the hold that had occurred after leaving Rio, recurred. He wrote from there in November 1903.

***

Dear parents and siblings,

Hopefully this letter finds you all as well as it leaves me. We, sadly, had a great stroke of hard luck. At present, the theater in Antofagasta is showing the burning of the Nesaia. With God's help, we survived the new and dreadful explosion. The captain's left hand is totally burned and five Chileans are hospitalized in Antofagasta. I will tell you what has happened: On Sunday, November 5 we were awakened at 11p.m to track coal gas in the ship because suddenly a noticeable heat was felt. It was approximately 40 degrees in the hold (40 deg.Celsius =105 Fahrenheit). By Monday morning, the heat was up to 55 degrees (131 Fahrenheit). On Monday we began searching for the fire. The coal was giving off so much gas that we finally could not continue to work, so the coals were wet down. In the night from Tuesday to Wednesday, we were again called out to seal the hatches. A heavy smoke was seeping out of the hold so we sealed them and engaged the extinguishing system. In the morning the captain went to Antofagasta to report the incident. Max and I and two lads were busy with the cables removing the last 16 bottles of carbolic acid when, at 10:30, we suddenly became aware of a deep rumble in the adjoining hold. Before we realized what it was, there was a terrible explosion. All three hatch covers were flung in the air and a tremendous column of flames shot up over our masts. How I got out of the cable hold I still don't know. When we got up on deck, almost everyone was already in the lifeboat. We wanted to go off the stern but the chief mate called to me that we should jump over the side at the bow and they would pick us up. But since nothing else seemed to be happening we all calmed down. The rest of the crew came back on board and we began to work as a matter of life and death. The hatches were made airtight with new canvas and the rest of the carbolic acid was pumped in. (I have not been able to find out why carbolic acid was pumped into the hold.)

A large lifeboat was lowered and everyone strapped on a cork vest, in case we should suddenly have to jump overboard. The captain was recalled by telegram and arrived at 3 p.m. At 4 p.m. the second explosion occurred. Fortunately no one was injured. The distress signal was raised and an old steamer arrived to pump water into the holds. A telegram was sent to Antofagasta for help. Half the crew manned the hand pumps and the other half threw the coal, which was lying on the deck, overboard. I was in the second group. We worked without letup for three days and three nights. The captain sent the chief mate ashore to bring local people on board to help so that we could get a few hours rest. It was about 9 p.m. when the mate arrived with workers. But they hadn't even boarded when another terrible explosion rocked the Nesaia. We saved ourselves by leaping overboard to avoid the huge column of flame but promptly climbed back on board to keep working. The Chileans lost their courage and, even though the captain offered them 100 dollars for three hours work, they abandoned us yelling, 'Nesaia is burning.' But we did not desert the ship. Now one can see what a German sailor can take.

We worked the entire night without let-up until 4 a.m. Every hour there was another explosion. We had practically given the Nesaia up when a rescue ship arrived from Antofagasta with 30 men to relieve us. We dropped where we stood and slept. From then on there were no more explosions. At noon a fire engine arrived from Antofagasta to wet down the Nesaia. Photographers also arrived and the danger appeared to be over. I commented to the chief mate, 'I wish these people were off the ship. If anything happens they will be the first ones off.' To compensate for their presence, these firefighters hauled away cases of Pilsner beer, wine, biscuits, sardines, etc. I climbed into my bunk at about 8 and immediately fell asleep. On the stern the firemen were drinking as though there was no tomorrow. At about 10, the captain said to the chief mate, 'Let's see if there is anymore fire.' He opened a hatch in the cabin and called the chief of the firemen over to get his opinion. This idiot, before the chief mate could stop him, lit a match. There had been no explosion for 16 hours and anyone, with any sense, could imagine the amount of coal gas that would have developed in a closed space with burning embers of coal. The chief mate told how he saw the blue flames run down the hold and, in that instant, the worst explosion to date occurred. The eight men in the cabin found themselves hurled up onto the deck. It's a miracle that no one was killed.

I was asleep in my bunk when the explosion aft occurred. I awakened and immediately jumped up on deck (in my underwear) and was met with bright flames. The main and aft hatch covers were tossed in the air, quickly followed by the forward hatch cover. A shutter flew past me just a handbreadth away. I jumped on the railing and made my way to the stern where two lads stood weeping. The Chileans were going crazy and howling that they were going to die. The entire fire company jumped on the barge and abandoned the ship. On the stern I met another sailor, who had not yet slept. He told me the captain and the chief mate had disappeared. We worked our way down to the cabin and I quickly pulled on a pair of pants and ran aft. Everywhere there were whimpering and wounded people. We finally found the captain; his whole left hand was burned as was his head and his beard. The chief mate had a chest wound but he quickly regained his senses. Most of our people had left the ship with the fire company. We went astern and found the entire cabin wrecked but not the cases with wine and beer. Everything was promptly consumed to keep the cowards from getting any. As a result, we got pretty happy.

On the afterdeck, we met a Chilean who had probably been knocked out. He was running around, waving a loaded pistol, and yelling for his companions. We took his gun away and would have gladly dumped him overboard if the captain hadn't calmed us down. We, again, worked the entire night and following day. Finally all the coals were under water and the fire was out. The fire engine left and only a watch of 20 Chileans and two officers remained on board. These were behaving in an extremely belligerent manner. We decided that if they went too far, we would throw them off the ship. We prepared for the coming night by arming ourselves with belaying pins [9] At 8 o'clock we laid down to sleep in the hope that we would finally be able to sleep through an entire night. For the rest, the wish was granted, but not for me. At 11, I was awakened out of a deep sleep by the chief mate, 'Erich, come out, it's happening. They are trying to take over our ship.' I went out ready to fight but the chief mate said it would be better to handle the situation calmly. Zistja, the man on watch, couldn't handle the upstarts alone and had, therefore, wakened the captain and the chief mate and requested a revolver. The captain and chief mate were now trying to calm the Chilean officer, but he declared bluntly, that he was now the captain of the Nesaia. He had orders to bring her to Antofagasta in the morning, since the ship had been salvaged through their efforts. The captain, however, disagreed since at no time had our entire crew left the ship. Had that occurred even once, they would have had the right.

The captain now gave me orders to guard this man since he threatened to again set the ship on fire. Then the captain went back to bed. Zistja and I watched. Once I caught one of the Chilean officers attempting to start a fire in the forward hold. I chased him away but immediately found him trying to do the same thing in the aft hold. By now, my patience was gone. I grabbed him by the neck and gave him a couple of good ones and he folded. I got my overcoat, covered him, and left him lying on the deck. When he regained his senses he was quite tame and offered us wine to make us drunk. However, he foolishly gave us sardines in oil to accompany the wine. He kept getting drunker and drunker but, thanks to the oil in the sardines, we remained sober. The fool thought he could get us drunk and we would fall asleep and they would get what they wanted...control of the Nesaia. When he realized his plan wouldn't work, he offered us money to go to sleep. In answer, I boxed his ears. I had previously thrown his revolver overboard. At 4 a.m., Zistja and I were relieved and went to sleep until 8 a.m. The following two nights were a repeat of the first. The captain went to the consulate and it was ordered that those 'demons' should leave the ship.

Now the assessment of damages by the insurance people got under way. The first assessment was for 200,000 Marks since the entire cargo was ruined. They were to go to Antofagasta to unload their ruined cargo and already had a tow arranged when they received word to wait for further instructions. This reminds me of that delightful cartoon "POGO©." In one episode Pogo finds a message tacked to a tree, "This is message one. Wait for message two." A little farther along he finds the second message, "This is message two, ignore message one." The continual change of orders must have been frustrating at best and downright aggravating at worst. Of the original 2800 tons of coal, 600 tons had been discharged before the explosions and fire so they still had to discharge 2200 tons somewhere.

"Where they will be discharged we do not know as yet. Every day orders arrive and they are always different. It will probably be

Whitsunday (the 7 Sunday after Easter) before we return, but it is just unfortunate and nothing can be done about it. We want to thank God that everything came out all right. One can judge the force of the explosions by the fact that one of the hatch covers was blown against an English ship anchored 500 meters (547 yards) away. Hopefully we will have better luck on the homeward journey. I feel sorry for the captain— his first trip as captain and so much hard luck. Recently he said he would give 1000 Taler [10] not to be captain now."*

The last entire letter was written on November 30, 1903. After his usual greeting to family and friends, he tells of receiving money for the first time since his arrival. With money in hand, several decided to walk to Antofagasta since there was nothing in Caleta Coloso.

"We did go, but never again would I attempt such a trek of my own free will. We had to cross a desert where we sank into the sand and the sun burned our heads until we thought we would go mad ... not a drop of water! The whole way was dotted with skeletal remains. We had to walk like this for approximately 10 hours. As we left the ship we took our dog with us. We had only been on the way for about half an hour when the poor thing went mad. Thick foam came from her mouth and she snapped wildly all around her so that we had to run away from her. I couldn't just leave her so I got near enough to give her two mighty blows on the head and put her out of her misery. We began unloading our cargo on Friday and the work continues at a good pace. I think we may still be able to leave before Christmas. We are supposed to take 600 tons to Iquique and there load saltpeter for Europe. I think we should be back by mid-May. I am really well but we do have to work hard. I am very pleased with the Nesaia. I hope that, this time, we will go to Germany."

There is one more partial letter from Iqique dated January 2, 1904, in which Erich described the damage to the ship and the false claim of the Chilean government that the ship had been abandoned by the crew. The Chileans had demanded 180,000 Mark for their "assistance and salvage." The crew signed affidavits contesting the claim, thereby saving the ship's owners a considerable sum of money. The ship had been so badly damaged by the explosions that the entire deck had to be torn up and replaced.   Naturally, the return home would be delayed by at least 6-8 weeks. And so his letters end.

The   odyssey of the *Nesaia* continued, albeit without Erich. She sailed with a load of coke from Rotterdam to Chile March 11, 1914, arriving in the harbor of Chanaral on June 27. She was interned for the duration of the war. In 1920 she was sent to Taltal and from there, on September 9, still under German flag, she sailed to Europe. After a journey of 177 days, she arrived in Hamburg on January 4, 1921 where she was granted to France for war reparations but never came under the French flag. In 1922 she was sold back to Germany and renamed *Barmen*. She sailed for five more years and was finally sold for scrap in May of 1925.

After the initial draft of this manuscript I was fortunate enough to find my grandfather's notebooks as well as one of my father's. The "Man Overboard" story was translated from father's notes as well as one about a Shipwreck that I have included in Part II.

Part Two

CAREER, FAMILY & WWI

URSULA McCAFFERTY

Chapter 6
Navy, School & Marriage

On October 1, 1904, Erich fulfilled another part of his dream. He attended Navigation School in Elsfleth, a town on the Weser River located NNW of Bremen. His studies lasted until May 29, 1905. He was then certified as "Seesteuermann auf Grosser Fahrt" (navigator of ocean-going vessels), making him a licensed "officer." While at school in Elsfleth, he met a seventeen-year-old blue-eyed tomboy named Kaetchen [11] Lichtenberg. Kate was the daughter of a sailing ship captain. Her mother had died when Kate was only seven years old so she had been raised and spoiled by neighbors. However, because these kind people considered vanity a sin, Kate was always told not to stand in front of a mirror because she was too homely. As a result, Kate couldn't understand why this dashing student kept following her around. Erich was absolutely smitten but it took a while before he captured Kate's heart.

In June, 1905 he was Chief Mate on a four-mast full-rigged ship, *Christine*. In September, 1906, he served as Third Mate on the Hansa steamer *Kuypfels* for a nine month trip to America, Africa, East Indies and back to Hamburg. On his return, Erich and Kate celebrated their engagement. His certification as Captain came after completion of the course from November 11th, 1907 through March 23rd, 1908. He had done it! One month shy of ten years the deckhand had achieved his goal and become a Master Mariner.

***

Erich's first Hansa Line uniform.

Erich's military obligation still needed to be fulfilled. He was granted leave from Hansa and served his mandatory time on the naval training vessel *Freya*. There is little detail available about his time aboard *Freya* except for the following account, written in Erich's own hand, about a collision of the *Freya* and an American schooner, *Maggie May*.

***

COLLISION
August 8, 1908

The weather is wonderful. Sunlight streams down on the blue waves of the Atlantic Ocean and on the large cruiser as it majestically makes its way through a sea barely rippled by wind. It is a warm summer day, a rarity here on the Newfoundland Bank, but there is an old adage, 'Don't praise the day before the evening,' and so it is now. At noon the wind dies down completely but on the distant horizon a great cloud is developing which is recognized by the experienced seamen as fog. All precautions are taken, and these are many, and the ship is rapidly engulfed in dense fog. Anyone never having experienced fog at sea, in heavily traveled waters, cannot imagine what it is like. It is an indescribable feeling. It makes one realize how helpless man can be at the mercy of nature. We have discovered X-Rays and we can send wireless messages over thousands of miles, but we have not developed rays to penetrate fog. Everything is shrouded in a gray haze and appears different than it actually is; this combined with dampness, creates a hush among the crew. Every two minutes the foghorn sounds eerily into the stillness surrounding us. The watch officer and the lookouts strain eyes and ears for any sound or shadow in the wall of fog that engulfs us. So it goes all day without change and without any parting in the dark gray wall. Night falls and all posts are doubled. Suddenly, at 11:30, the Commandant who is on the command bridge along with the watch officer, notices a shadow just off the larboard [12] side. At the same time they hear someone shouting. Immediately the rudder is turned sharply to starboard [12], but too late. With a terrible crash the bowsprit of the cruiser tears into the schooner. Not for a moment does the captain lose

69

his wits; he orders, 'Stop engines! All lifeboat crews and firemen to their stations!' Immediately the boatswains whistle shrills throughout the ship and the men tumble out, clad only in their underwear, and rush to their respective stations. The boats cannot be lowered while the unfortunate ship is still speared on the bowsprit of the cruiser. No one knows if the schooner will immediately sink when it pulls free or if it will float alongside until the lifeboats can reach it.

From the foredeck the crew sees a sad picture, one they will never be able to forget. Floodlights and flares light the scene. The American schooner, (which this vessel is), has been rammed by the sharp bowsprit of the Freya behind the foredeck and sliced in two. The captain of the schooner is standing on the steps of the afterdeck and is holding high a blue flare. His crew hurries to the rear to seek safety, since their lifeboats have been destroyed by the collision.

Instinctively they head for their leader who, unfortunately, is also powerless. Suddenly the masts collapse and the huge sails fall, engulfing all beneath, and the entire unfortunate vessel plunges down into the depths. Now a heartrending scene plays out...the captain, maintaining his place and still holding high the blue flare, sinks into the sea. At the last minute, a few of the crew manage to leap off the ship. Now they struggle to avoid death in the sea. Over there drifts a man; he has a barrel near him and is attempting to hold onto it and is calling, in German, 'For God's sake help me, my mother, my mother.'

He doesn't have to call any longer because as soon as the schooner has sunk, the cruiser immediately lowers the lifeboats in order to rescue whomever they can. For the German sailor it is too late. Just as the lifeboat nears him he sinks out of sight. Over there are two brothers (Canadians) calling for their father and brother who have evidently gone down with the schooner. One is violently cursing in fear of dying and at the ship that has brought them so close to death. These two, a third Canadian and an American, are rescued by the lifeboats and immediately brought onboard where they are warmly greeted.

The boats set out again and search throughout the night at the tragic scene. No other survivors are found. Of the thirteen men aboard, only four are saved. This includes the two who lost their father and their brother in the collision. Aboard the Freya, everything possible is done for the survivors. They are supplied with clothing and with the deep sympathy that only a fellow seaman can give.

The next day the weather is fine again with no trace of the deadly fog. The Freya makes port in Halifax to put the survivors ashore, but before they leave they are   presented with a purse collected by the crew of the Freya. With sorrowful but grateful hearts they leave the ship that, unintentionally, caused them so much grief.

Erich on the naval training ship Freya.

After completing his year in the navy, Erich returned to work with the Hansa Company. On June 28, 1910, he and Kate were married in Sundhausen with Erich's father, Pastor Robert Richter, officiating.

Kaetchen Lichtenberg and Erich Richter
(En route to the Registrars office to
apply for their marriage license)

They settled into what should have been a comfortable, financially secure life. Erich's career was established, and he had found his true love. Who could wish for more? His career as a ship's officer for the "Hansa" line out of Bremen was all that he could have wished for. Kate had grown up in a seafaring household and was well prepared for the long separations.

On July 20, 1910, Erich was temporarily promoted to 2nd Mate on the *Fangsturm*. The young couple was reunited for Christmas. Erich was then assigned as Third Mate on the

Arstorturm for one trip. In the same month Erich was permanently promoted to Second Mate. He remained in that position on the *Arsterturm* until March, 1912, and then transferred to the *Wartenfels*.

On April 11, 1922, Kate gave birth to their first child, Olga Margarete Helene Richter. Erich saw his daughter for the first time in October, 1911, when she was six months old. Kate placed the baby in his arms and as soon as she left the room he handed the baby to his sister-in-law, commenting that he was afraid he would break the baby's tiny limbs.

By December he had already been promoted to Chief Mate, and in 1913 he became Chief Mate on the *Tannenfels*. The ship was scheduled to go on a long trip and not expected home until October 1914. On December 13, 1913, Kate gave birth to a son, Erich Robert Richter, and Erich looked forward to being home in time to celebrate his son's first birthday.

1913: Aboard the Tannenfels.
Erich is seated far right.

Chapter 7
POW

There would be no "first birthday" reunion. At the outbreak of WWI in June of 1914, the *Tannenfels* was designated as a supply ship for the German navy. The return home would be delayed. They were en route to supply the battleship *Emden* on October 18, 1914, when the *Tannenfels* was captured in the Basilan Strait, Philippines by the British destroyer *HMS Chelmer*. All aboard were interned as prisoners of war.

They were first taken to Hong Kong and then shipped to Australia. The prisoner of war camp was established in an old prison complex at Berrima, Australia, southwest of Sydney. This was a civilian POW camp and included mostly seafaring men and the families that had been traveling with them- - -wives and even children. For a time, conditions were harsh, food limited and mutton was the meat of choice. To his dying day Erich refused to allow lamb in the house because he couldn't stand the smell. It probably brought back memories best forgotten. Being a prisoner of war can never be a pleasant situation, but one wonders how much more the lack of freedom chafed among these men who were used to the open sea.

Location of Basilan Strait
and capture of the *Tannenfels*

When the *Tannenfels* was captured, Erich weighed close to 200 pounds, a big man standing six feet tall. As the war dragged on, year after long year, the only redeeming feature of the incarceration was that no one was shooting at the prisoners. The physical condition of the prisoners was a different story indeed; living conditions were less than satisfactory. During wars hatred runs high and they were certainly targets of that... the detested "Bosch." They received mail and photos from home, but one commander of the camp had a sadisitic streak and actually tore up one of the photos that Kate sent to Erich, in Erich's presence. Erich never forgot that little bit of cruelty. He was so angry that he vowed to hunt this man down after the war. Fortunately the man was transferred and Erich's rage abated. It was the photos of his beloved Kate and the children that kept his spirits up.

However, Erich's great concern about the welfare of his family certainly was also a contributing factor to his weight loss. During the war, Kate and the children's diets were also lacking. Kate's notes state that they were rationed fifty grams each of fat and meat per week (one ounce is twenty-three grams). Photos taken of Kate and the children in 1913 and early 1914 are quite different from the pictures taken in 1915. This must have been very stressful for Erich. One can only imagine the sense of helplessness that engulfed him and his fellow prisoners. At times they surely must have despaired of ever seeing their loved ones again. It was strength in numbers that allowed them all to survive until their final release and repatriation. The men whose families had accompanied them and were interned with them, at least had the consolation of knowing how their loved ones were faring. Not so for the men who were reparated so long a time from their wives and children.

The following pictures were taken over the years between 1914 and 1919. The Berrima photos show the gradual changes in Erich. The photos that Kate sent to him show the gradual change in her and the children.

***

POW Photos
In this photo it appears that the prisoners were growing pole beans. Erich is far right.

The camp at Berrima, Australia
Erich is in the back row center in gray.

***

Erich and a fellow prisoner in Berrima, Australia.
Behind them the large walls surrounding the prison are
visible.

***

Entrance to Berrrima Prison: Courtesy Australian War
Memorial

***

The photos taken in Berrima are all in the form of post
cards and on two Erich wrote dates and comments. The
photo with the pole beans is addressed to Kate in Bremen
on the 6th of February, 1918 and signed, *"Your faithful Erich."*
On the back of the following one he had written the
following message: *"A day will come for us, a day bright and
clear.*

***

The sign says *"Prisoners of war of the
HANSA Line, BERRIMA June 1917."*
Erich is the last man on the right in the last row.

***

The following photographs are those that Kate sent to
Erich.

***

Kate and daughter Olga circa 1913

Kate and Erich Jr. in early 1914

Olga, Erich Jr, and Kate in 1915
Kate's face is already thinner.

Erich Jr., Kate and Olga, 1916
Even Olga looks thinner.

Chapter 8
Homecoming

In December of 1919 or January of 1920, Erich finally came home. He weighed 120 pounds. His young son was already six years old, and the daughter he had left as a toddler was almost nine. His beloved Kate was a shadow of her former self and weighed only 97 pounds; both were physical and nervous wrecks. The doctor told Kate that she needed to get Erich out among people in order to readjust to normal life. He was gaunt and weary, the consummate sailor that he was, who had come home to a country that no longer had a merchant fleet. Most of Germany's ships were assigned to the Allies for war reparations. The former shipping giant, Hansa, could offer him no work but did give him an excellent recommendation. They assured him they would certainly rehire him, should the situation change. The original recommendation, dated March 27, 1922 is in German but it translates as follows:

"We certify herewith, that Mr. Erich Richter, born Aug 14, 1882, from August of 1906 until the start of the war, served as 3rd, 2nd, and 1st officer on various steamers, lastly on the TANNENFELS which was captured by the British in 1914. The crew was taken prisoner of war. During his entire employment with us, Mr. Richter established himself as responsible, sober, dependable and exemplary. His captains highly recommended his ability as a navigator. They also praised his honesty and trustworthiness. We regret that, at present, we are unable to rehire him, since we no longer have a fleet, but should the situation change, we would certainly place him again."

Although a glowing reference is always welcome, it does not put bread on the table; Erich now had a wife and two children to support. He had been home just a little over a month when Kate developed a severe kidney infection and was hospitalized for five long weeks. When she was finally on the mend she encouraged Erich to go to Sundhausen to visit his mother. His father had died in March of 1914 and Erich hadn't been home since before the war. Although his health had improved somewhat during his visit home, he still fretted because there were no ships. He had no work from October 1919 until his brother Robert managed to get him a job as a warehouse manager. The job included an apartment above the warehouse.

They settled into a strange new life and Erich tried to become a "landlubber." He joined the "Liederkranz" (a singing society). The warehouse stocked food supplies from America that were distributed to hard laborers such as factory workers and steel workers. As manager, Erich received ample rations for his family. His employers supplied him with a revolver so that he could prevent theft and protect himself.

In October of 1920, I was born and the family numbered five. But Erich was restless and longed for the open sea. He had been confined for long years ashore in a strange land and now he was trapped in a shore job he hated. He began to drink and at the same time to hate himself for being weak. He told Kate he had to get out of there. All his spare time was spent in looking for any work that dealt with ships.

One day he came home and told Kate that a foreign ship in the harbor wanted a man with a navigators license to stand watch while the officers took shore leave. Erich went to his employer and asked him to find a replacement for the warehouse. Fortunately, the man they hired had a nice apartment in Hamburg and was willing to trade with Erich and Kate. Erich was much happier but still longed to go back to sea.

One evening he came home and asked Kate how she would feel about his going to America. She told him he would have to first go alone, working his way over, because all their savings were gone and there was no money for passage. He assured her that there was no cause to worry because he could get a job on a former German ship that had been awarded to the Americans and was now under Panamanian flag. The American engineers didn't like the German engines and the American Officers did not want to sail with German engineers. As a result, the owners were trying to get German engineers and officers to sail their ships.

Erich told Kate that he had heard about this opportunity too late to try for the Chief Mate's job but that he would try for the position of Second Mate. Any officer's job with American wages would be better than the inflated German currency.

He applied for the position of Second Mate on Monday but needed to have all his papers in order by Wednesday noon. Erich went to the American consulate and had no problems getting the documentation he needed. Kate headed for the German authorities to obtain a sailing permit for Erich. She was told it would be ready on Wednesday afternoon. She told them that Wednesday afternoon would be too late, but they explained that getting it any earlier would require special messengers and that was expensive. The stamp that was required cost only twenty Mark so Kate placed a 100 Mark bill into Erich's passport and passed it back to the clerk. She was told that she could pick up the documents later that day.

Erich got his job and sailed as a passenger to New York on the following day to meet the ship and begin his duties as Second Mate. Once on board, in September 1922, the man hired as Chief Mate didn't feel he had enough experience to fill the position so he asked Erich to trade jobs with him. Erich sailed under Panamanian flag for nine months. Then the former German owner bought the ship back.

The family was financially well off now because Erich was paid in American dollars while the German Mark's value kept plummeting. In 1923 Kate went to Naples to meet

Erich's ship. The trip from Hamburg to Naples cost her five American dollars. When she arrived in Naples she found out that Erich's ship was not coming through the Suez Canal as expected but was coming around the Cape of Good Hope instead. They had a cargo of wheat and the owners saw that the price of wheat was climbing and therefore delayed the arrival to get the best price. Kate waited in Naples for five weeks before Erich arrived. He didn't know that she was in Naples and she didn't know that the ship was destined for England instead of Germany. She had planned to sail home with Erich. After a nice holiday in sunny Naples, Kate managed to convince the American captain that she was a pretty good sailor and, since he couldn't carry her as a passenger, he "hired" her as a stewardess for one dollar per month. In her notes Kate described it as a lovely trip across the blue Mediterranean and on to Cardiff. In Cardiff the German crew came aboard and Erich was asked to stay on until Bremen.

There were quite a few German licensed officers who had not been able to get work since the end of the war, and the owners asked Erich to stay on as a Second Mate to give some of the others a chance at the higher positions. But Erich wanted to go home and see his family and make some serious decisions. He didn't want to rush into things but he did want to buy a home in either Hamburg or Bremen. He had nine months wages in American dollars and the safest investment would certainly have been property. The inflation had devalued the Mark so much that one American dollar was worth a billion Mark. Kate warned Erich not to show any American currency and, on her advice, he took one twenty-dollar bill and exchanged it at the bank.

The next day they planned a trip to Kate's hometown of Elsfleth. When they arrived at the railroad station she went into the restaurant to order breakfast while Erich bought their tickets. He joined Kate in the dining room and when he sat down he turned ghastly pale. Kate asked him what was wrong and he said, *"My God, my wallet with the American dollars is gone."* They alerted the railroad detective but had no luck in retrieving the wallet. They cancelled their trip to Elsfleth and notified a couple of Erich's shipmates. One of them came to the station and when he heard what had happened he asked Kate how she could be so calm. She told him there was no point in crying over spilled milk.

Erich was very upset and wanted to go right to Bremen and take any job, Second or Third Mate, anything he could find. Kate dissuaded him. She suggested that he should do what he really wanted to do, go back to America and earn the money again. Then, as soon as he had earned enough to send for her, she would leave the children with her sister and go to America too. They could then both work to earn the money for passage for the children and Kate's sister. Kate thought that, in America, people were used to having money and wouldn't need to steal.

Part Three

AMERICA

Chapter 9
A New Beginning

When Erich arrived in New York he tried to contact his former employers but they had gone out of business. There he was in New York, family in Germany, and almost penniless. He took any job he could find as long as it dealt with ships. He worked as a longshoreman but he wasn't wanted because he didn't speak their language. Then he got a job on a lumber barge earning $28.50 a week but took his cargo on consignment; that enabled him to make a small profit on each load. It was hard labor, but he was looking forward to becoming a citizen in five years; then he would again be able to sail as a ship's officer.

Late one night, when the barge had been towed to a pier in New York City, Erich had an accident. A hawser (heavy line) caught around the top joint of the middle finger of his right hand, and almost tore the joint off. It was late and Erich knew no one, so he wandered around the streets looking for help. Someone finally directed him to a doctor's office and the dangling joint was amputated. The doctor had no anesthesia but he did have whiskey. The whiskey served a two-fold purpose—it sterilized the wound and enough was pumped into Erich to help deaden the pain. Somehow he found his way back to his barge and collapsed in a heap in his bunk. He had a raging fever for several days but soon he was able to function again. Many years later he told me that he always knew when bad weather was coming because the missing joint of his finger ached. How anyone who suffered so many disasters could still maintain a sense of humor and a love of music and poetry is a cause of wonder for me.

Kate had wanted to join Erich in 1924 but the American Immigration doctor in Germany rejected her. She finally arrived in January of 1925. Erich actually had borrowed some money to pay her passage. He had rented a furnished room in a boarding house, a room he had only seen at night. Kate quickly found out that daylight only reached the room for two hours each afternoon. In this gloom and with Erich away all day, Kate soon became very homesick for her family and her nice bright apartment in Hamburg.

The landlady informed Kate that boarders were not supposed to be home during the day. She told Kate she should get a job. Kate asked what kind of job she could get when she didn't speak English. But the landlady had an easy answer; she told Kate to do housework for Jewish families since most of them understood German. Kate did just that and after three days she was so weak that she couldn't hold her fork at dinner. She was still exceedingly undernourished and her employers had her work for twelve hours without providing any food. When Erich found out that Kate was cleaning for other people, he was furious and made her quit then and there. Her problem was attitude; when told to clean a room she cleaned it from top to bottom the way one does for spring-cleaning. She tried one more cleaning job but when Erich came home he made her quit that also. Eventually she found a job with a perfume manufacturer. The owners spoke German so language was no problem and Kate really enjoyed the work and her fellow employees. One of the perfumes they were bottling was lily-of-the-valley that Kate pronounced *"Lie-lie-de-vie-lie."* She was teased about that for years to come.

Her salary was $18 a week and was later raised to $19. Her hours were from 9 a.m. to 5 p.m. so she was able to cook dinner for Erich when he came home. Their joint income was $47 per week and this had to support the family in Germany and Kate and Erich in New York. Fortunately they received 1000 Mark from the German government for the war losses Erich had suffered. By now the Mark was stabilized and they were able to send for their family in November of 1925.

The children and Kate's sister Hedwig arrived in New York after a very rough Atlantic crossing on the old *Bremen*. In the 1930s a fast, new ship was also named *Bremen* but the one the family traveled on was an old and weary ship and was nearly lost during a violent storm on the crossing. That particular North Atlantic storm was so severe that the New York Daily News featured photos of waves breaking over the deck. I'm not sure if the man who took the photos was a journalist or not. I remember people discussing the man who went on deck at the height of the storm to take photos and that he had fallen and broken his leg.

They found an apartment in a lovely old brownstone in the Bay Ridge section of Brooklyn. They bought the essential furniture "on time"- enough beds, a kitchen table and chairs and a dining room table and chairs. Erich worked hard and his lumber consignment work paid well so they were soon able to pay off what they owed. By then they had learned a lot and bought the balance of their furniture second-hand and paid cash.

The family settled into a new life and the "Americanization" of the children began. Young Erich, who was gregarious and outgoing, quickly made friends with neighborhood boys, so the language barrier was overcome in short order. He was happy-go-lucky and allowed me, the "Kid" (a nickname that stuck with me into adulthood and beyond), to tag along on his adventures. The boys created an imaginary "wilderness" in the empty lot on the corner of our block and there they roasted "mickies" (potatoes purloined from our families' pantries) in an open fire. They were usually pretty black on the outside and pretty raw in the middle but it was the ambience that made them special.

Things were tougher for big sister Olga. She had begun high school before leaving Hamburg and, because she spoke no English, was placed in the first grade in school. This was a different time in America, immigrants were expected to learn English and were NOT taught in their native tongue in public schools. Olga was horrified. Not only was she 14, she was a tall 14. The younger children taunted her and she grimly stuck it out as long as the law required, but at 16, she quit school and went to work. She never really found total peace in the USA and always yearned for her "homeland."

Brother Erich and I quickly became "American," but for our father Erich things were again changing.

The owners of the barge company began dealing in pig iron instead of lumber and the work became much harder. Erich had to put in seventy hours each week in order to make ends meet. Kate stayed home with the family. She and aunt Hedwig earned money to supplement the family income doing "homework." At the time, homework was a very common way for women to earn a modest income. It usually entailed sewing pre-cut garments or embroidering and adding other finishing touches on garments. The work was distributed at a factory and completed at home, allowing mothers to be at home with their children and still be able to earn a few extra dollars. The manufacturer did not have to supply loft space with dozens of sewing machines, thereby cutting costs dramatically. However, even with Kate and Hedwig's help, money was short. The rent on the apartment was more than they could continue to pay, so the family moved in 1927.

Erich was acquainted with an old retired German sea captain who owned a large house in the Dyker Heights section of Brooklyn. The attic of the house had been converted into an apartment for the captain's daughter and her husband. They were an upwardly mobile couple and were anxious to live in an upscale community in Scarsdale, N.Y. As soon as they were financially able she and her husband bought a new home and the apartment became available.

Since the only access to the apartment was through the captain's residence, he didn't want to rent it to strangers. The rent was $35 per month with gas and electric included. This was a saving on the rent alone of $30 per month. In 1927 that was a substantial saving. The apartment consisted of a dining area, kitchen, living room, two bedrooms (one very tiny one), a wide hall, and a bathroom. Aunt Hedwig was no longer living with us, so our parents took the larger bedroom; Olga and I shared the tiny one. Brother Erich had his bed in a nook under the eaves off the hall. If money was short, the rent was cheap and when it was really short, the rent could wait and often did. The arrangement was certainly a mixed blessing. We had a place to live but were always being watched and observed and judged by the landlord. He never considered that he was interfering in our personal privacy. Olga and I grew to hate him with a passion. Brother Erich went off to sea after high school so he didn't care. Olga and I each "escaped" when we married, and our parents finally moved out in 1942.

Kate talked Erich into leaving the pig iron barge because the work was too hard. The economy was bad just before the depression and Erich took a job on a cement barge earning $90 per month. Erich Jr. took a summer job while he was in high school and Olga was already working. They both contributed to the household expenses. During the summer vacations, Kate and I, the youngest, spent time on the barge with Erich. I thought it was grand to be in tow, in a string of barges, gliding down the mighty Hudson River. Although it was an idyllic vacation for a child, it was certainly not the work for which Erich had trained and worked so hard to achieve. He longed for the command of a real ship and to again be sailing the oceans.

In 1929 Erich had fulfilled his five-year residency requirement and applied for citizenship. Instead of getting his papers he was told that he had to go back to Germany and re-enter the country under the quota. The problem stemmed from the fact that when he worked his way across in 1924, no one had told him that he was required to pay a head tax. Without his citizenship papers he could not be licensed as an American officer in spite of the fact that he had German certification and years of experience.

Erich told his troubles to a shipping agent who managed to get him a job on an American ship that was sold to Germany to be scrapped. The ship was put under German flag so Erich was finally able to go back to his sea.

Chapter 10
Columbia

In 1932, he was hired as captain of an American yacht, the *Flying Fox* which had been converted to a gunship for the Columbian navy and renamed the *Mariscal Sucre*. Columbia was at war with Peru and the *Mariscal Sucre* was dispatched from New York to her station on the Putamyo River.

***

Aboard the Mariscal Sucre
l-r· Lt, & Mrs. Diego, Erich, bride of & Lt. Castro, wife of photographer.

***

Flagship of the Colombian Navy Mariscal Sucre
(formerly the yacht of W.B. Leeds - *The Flying Fox)*

The Putamayo River winds its way through jungles and forms a good part of the border between Colombia and Peru. Erich told of wild animals along the shore, of natives they met along the way and of the piranhas in the water. One Colombian soldier lost his life because of the deadly piranhas. As he was boarding the ship, he slipped and fell into the water. Even though he was quickly pulled out, his legs had been so badly bitten by the carnivorous fish that he bled to death in minutes. Erich particularly enjoyed meeting the native people. The women were delighted to receive, of all things, men's undershirts, which they donned with great pride. And he spoke of seeing different apes in the trees and laughing at their antics. Had it not been a war situation, this whole experience on the Putamayo River would have been sheer adventure.

While Erich was based in Cartagena, Kate was able to join him for several months. She rented temporary accommodations in a boarding house that, unknown to the owner, had acquired the nickname of "House of the Vultures" because there were always several of the ugly beasts sitting on the roof. Although the landlady was a jovial soul, from Kate's description one must assume that keeping a sanitary kitchen was not one of her prime aims in life.

Erich's position afforded them a gracious life style and a new circle of friends, an enjoyable experience after the long, hungry years of WWI, and the struggle to create a new home in America.

After a several month visit, Kate returned home to Brooklyn, and with the cessation of hostilities, Erich returned home via passenger ship. While on board, he was bitten by a scorpion and collapsed in the dining room. Quick action by the ship's doctor saved his life. He received another satisfactory reference from the Inspector General of the Colombian navy. The original document is fragile and does not scan well so I have copied the certified translation herewith:

***

Navy of Colombia, Cruiser Mariscal Sucre,
Office of the Commander

The undersigned Inspector—General of the War Fleet, in campaign in the waters of the Putumayo River and its tributaries, herewith certifies that Captain Erich Richter has served as Captain of the Cruiser Mariscal Sucre since the said cruiser sailed from the roadway of New York until the date on which Peace was declared between Peru and Colombia. This Office takes pleasure in acknowledging the expertness, honorability and determination with which Captain Richter performed the duties of his Office.

Bocas del rio Algodon, Putumayo River, May 25, 1933
Signed: Carlos Cortes Vayas, Inspector General.

Chapter 11
Back in Brooklyn

After Colombia, Erich worked for a time as a pier superintendent, at the Bush Terminal in Brooklyn, where the sleek, new *Bremen* and *Europa* were berthed when in New York. Finally, on January 7, 1936, Erich proudly swore allegiance to the United States of America and became a citizen. Kate had become a citizen in 1933 as had the children. Now life really began to improve. Erich took all the necessary exams to obtain his American certification and once more was in his element. He made the rounds of all shipping companies and brokerage houses looking for anything in his line of work. The economy was not good and jobs were not that easy to find. Erich made contact with a shipping broker named Frederick Zimmerman. Mr. Zimmerman was in the business of buying and selling ships and required crews, from time to time, to move his ships from one port to another. Since he was not a full fledged shipping company he hired crews as needed and for short terms. He was impressed with Erich's record and recommendations and hired him from time to time whenever he was available.

The following is a copy of one of Mr. Zimmermann's appointments:

***

F.L. Zimmerman & Co., LTD
SHIP BROKERS
24 STATE STREET
NEW YORK, N.Y., USA

Captain Erich Richter,
1215-85th Street,
Brooklyn, N.Y.

Dear Captain,

You are herewith instructed to proceed tonight to Portland, ME, and to take there possession of the steamer *Mayan,* which I just purchased from the Trustee, Judge William W. Dey, of the Atlantic States Transportation Co., Inc. in bankruptcy of Norfolk, Va. by order of the Federal Court at Norfolk, Va.

Please take immediately inventory and send me a copy and make a full report about the condition of the steamer as soon as possible and attend to all matters according to your best judgment.

Yours very truly
FREDERICK L ZIMMERMANN
FLZ/AA

***

This letter was followed by another, dated August 24th, 1937, in which F. Zimmermann certifies that Erich was captain of the steamer *Mayan* from the beginning of May until sold in July. He further states that as soon as he had another opening for Erich he would get in touch as his services were always exceptionally satisfactory. I remember one of the other ships, for which Mr. Zimermann hired Erich. She was named *Ruth.*

Any work Erich did for the shipping broker paid very well and for Kate this was a special treat. She had always had nice things when growing up and longed to dress her family well. While Erich was on the *Ruth,* I remember being taken to Altman's Department Store in New York and being outfitted from head to foot in a navy blue pleated skirt, a white blouse and a navy blue sweater and new shoes and socks. Erich was so proud when he was able to provide the nicer things for his family. Unfortunately, the work for Mr. Zimmerman was not steady and it became a case of feast or famine.

As a result, Erich worked many different jobs.

***

Erich and Kate Aboard Ruth, 1932

***

A letter dated May 15, 1939 is an example of the sort of work Erich would do and what he could earn. I was surprised to note that all three of his initials were used. Since his earliest letters he never referred to himself as anything but Erich and he never signed anything with the name Gustav.

***

"To Whom It May Concern"

This will confirm an arrangement between Captain Johnson of the M.V. Douglas Alexander, owned by the Government of Bahamas, and Captain G.A.E. Richter of New York as follows:

Captain Richter will join M.V. Douglas Alexander as a Sea Pilot and proceed with the ship from New York to Cape May outside thence inside route through Chesapeake and Delaware Canal, Chesapeake Bay and then follow inside route to Beaufort, N.C., then follow Coast to Jacksonville.

Captain Richter's remuneration will be $125.00 and his rail will be paid from Jacksonville back to New York.

In the 21st century, one can hardly believe that anyone would undertake such responsibility, and lend such expertise to any project for $125.00, but in 1939 this was a respectable wage. In 1939 I worked as a file clerk in a large corporation and was happy to be paid $65 per month.

There were, of course, periods of unemployment. Those occasionally produced dark and moody days for Erich. He brooded and paced the floor or sat at the table playing solitaire. Everyone walked around on tiptoes in order to avoid drawing his attention. When he was frustrated at not having work he tended to let his frustrations out on the first one to cross his path. This usually amounted to a lecture about some misdeed or failure to finish a chore.

Kate would warn the children to tread lightly because *"Your father is in a bad mood."* Kate finally put an end to these black moods herself. Once, as Erich sat playing solitaire and looking grim, she marched over to the table, slammed her fist down among his cards, scattering them in all directions, and informed him that she no longer intended to put up with such nonsense. A shocked (and chastened) Erich commented, *"You have become very American."* I don't remember ever seeing him in a black mood again. If he worried he just paced back and forth as though he were walking the bridge of a ship.

It wasn't always dark and gloomy when Erich was home because he loved music and enjoyed a good laugh along with everyone else. In fact, at times, he had a wicked sense of mischief. We had a "Victrola," a handsome brown cabinet with a crank handle and with a covered turntable. It played 78 rpm records, but you had to keep it cranked up or the music would slow down. Erich loved marches and played them at full volume, his favorite (and mine) being the Radetsky March by Johann Strauss the elder. Other favorites were records of the great Enrico Caruso. We played games like 500 rummy and Parchesi and Erich taught me solitaire at an early age.

When there was no ship there was no salary. The grocery store at the end of our street was a "Mom & Pop" store and, because they too had faced hard times, they graciously ran a tab for us. I guess they realized that as soon as Erich had another ship, their bill would be the first one to be paid. In the interim Kate cooked hardy, cheap meals. At the time beef tongue was NOT a delicacy and she managed to get three meals out of one tongue, the third meal being hash. Stuffed peppers, cabbage cooked with a piece of smoked bacon for flavor, and one of my favorites...potato pancakes with applesauce-- were also budget stretchers. But being poor was not a disgrace in the thirties. Erich never had to stand on a street corner and sell apples or shovel snow off city streets. During the Great Depression, many a family man had to do just that—sell apples and shovel snow.

When Erich did have a ship and it was due to make port along the eastern seaboard, be it Boston or Baltimore or any points in between, whenever possible, Kate made it a point to be on the pier waiting for him when the ship docked. In September of 1938 she was recuperating from major surgery but Erich was due in Fall River, Massachusetts. The great New England hurricane hit on September 21. Two days later Kate set off by train for Fall River. When the train reached New Haven, Connecticut, everyone was transferred to buses. The train tracks along the coast were littered with debris and stranded boats.

Kate made it to Fall River only to find that the pier had been washed away and Erich would be docking in Chelsea in the Boston area. I never did find out just how she got as far as the MTA in Boston late at night. She was weary and a little feverish and decided to find a hotel. She left the MTA at the Scully Square station and asked the lady in the change booth where she might find accommodations. She had been traveling for hours on end and probably looked like less than the lady she was. She was directed to a hotel just up the street from the station, the Crawford House. Kate was not so naïve that she didn't immediately recognize the hotel as catering to "working girls." She was too exhausted to care, locked herself in her room and went to bed. In the morning she phoned the pier and left a message for Erich giving only the phone number, not the name of the hotel. It wasn't long before Erich phoned and demanded to know what she was doing in the Crawford House. It seems that the phone number was well known by the men in the pier office. Kate was told to stay in the room and Erich "rescued" her. He was embarrassed to be seen both entering and leaving the establishment. The irony was that the respectable Palmer House was just one block away.

By now, Erich Jr. was already a seafaring man. He was plying the Atlantic coast from New York to Texas on oil tankers and aiming for an eventual command of his own. Daughter Olga was married and living in Manhattan. She and her husband had returned to Germany to live but she had awakened one night to loud rumblings in the street. When she looked out she saw tanks rolling through the town. The writing was on the wall; they packed up their belongings and came home to America.

We watched as Europe went through the agonies of war and prayed that it would soon be over. I married in July of 1941 and then, on December 7, our whole lives turned upside down.

Part Four

WORLD WAR II

Chapter 12
Accusations

In December of 1940, Erich signed on with the Marine Transport Company. Once the United States was officially at war, the need for ships and men to sail them became a priority. Not only were the ships needed to ferry supplies to the war front, but they were also required to transport our troops. Now there was no shortage of work for Erich. Everything was going well for him. He was again a ship's officer, earning good money and doing what he loved best. But Fate just had to throw a little twist into his life.

In 1942 the war was raging. Feelings and emotions were running high, so everything German or Japanese became suspect. I was working in a large office in New York and my Jewish co-workers refused to sit with me in the cafeteria. Japanese-Americans were sent to camps. To be an object of hatred through no fault or sin of your own can be painful indeed. In Erich's case it became not only hurtful, but an economic burden as well. At the time, Erich was Second Officer on the *Swift Arrow*. The ship was in Baltimore loading cargo, and Erich, dressed in his khaki work uniform, was arrested and taken off his ship at gunpoint, accused of being a Nazi spy.

He was absolutely devastated and confused. And then the story came to light. One of the crew had come back on board after liberty in a very intoxicated state. Erich had no patience with drunkenness and read the sailor the riot act. The sailor, a small –minded man, wanted to get even. He chose a unique way of doing so. He contacted Naval Intelligence and "informed" on Erich, accusing him of being a Nazi. Nothing could have been further from the truth. Erich had been to Germany on various ships after Hitler first came to power and he was appalled by what was happening

115

in Germany. He was convinced that Hitler was a madman and made no bones about his opinion. However, since the accusation was made and the climate was strictly unfriendly, Erich was interrogated. A bandage he had on that covered a cut on his shin was removed in a search for microfilm, and then he was sent home to await the outcome of the investigation. It was ludicrous. My brother, Erich, was captain of an oil tanker plying the Atlantic coast, and oil tankers were prime targets of U-boats. Why would my father choose to aid and abet an enemy that was torpedoing American ships when both he and my brother were sailing those ships?

Unfortunately, when you don't work you don't get paid. The investigation seemed to drag on and on. The FBI paid Erich and Kate a visit. Although they were extremely polite, it was still a very unpleasant situation to have strangers pawing through bureau drawers and personal papers.

Although I was married and no longer living at home, I could see how hurt my father was. He had sworn allegiance to this country; he was an honorable man who did not take such things lightly. The fact that his loyalty was questioned was, by far, more painful than losing his income.

Having grown up as an American, I was convinced that justice would prevail and that it was legal and proper to rebut the charges made. I knew the name of the Lieutenant in charge of my father's case and I phoned his office. I was informed that the Lieutenant was on leave. I asked who was handling his caseload in his absence and was told that his files were locked in his desk and no one was working on his cases while he was away. I was more than a little perturbed. I sat down and typed a letter to President Roosevelt and complained bitterly about the injustice heaped on my father. Miraculously, within a week, Erich received a letter from someone on the White House staff directing him to contact a gentleman who was head of an organization named, "Loyal

Americans of German Descent." After a quick conference, Erich was cleared of all charges and was able to resume his work as a Chief Mate on the *M /V Panam*. I recently tried to find details of the investigation. Naval Intelligence was not able to help me; a letter to the President led to a referral to the National Archives:

***

National Archives and Records Administration

8601 Adelphi Road
College Park, Maryland 20740-6001
November 7, 2003

Mrs. Ursula McCafferty P.O. Box 325
Canaan, CT 06018-0325

   This is in response to your letter of October 20, 2003 in which you requested that a search be conducted for any information relating to your father, Captain Erich Richter. A search was conducted among the general records of the Department of Justice, specifically the "General Index," 1928-51 and we located an indices card for Erich Richter that indicates that a Department of Justice case file, numbered 146-43-742 was opened on August 15, 1942. We checked among our Department of Justice holdings but the aforementioned file is not part of our holdings. We regret that we were unable to locate any additional information relative to your request.

Sincerely,
FRED ROMANSKI
Archivist, Civilian Records
Textual Archives Services Division

117

Chapter 13
Wolf Packs

By 1943, the North Atlantic was becoming a suicide run because of the "wolf pack" [13] submarine attacks. Erich made the North Atlantic crossing in huge convoys. On April 11, the night of my sister's birthday, one such convoy came under attack from a wolf pack. It was a wild night with up to 13 ships being damaged or sunk. Erich described it as a madhouse; ships on the perimeter of the convoy tried to steer to the center; gun crews on all the ships were firing in an effort to discourage the submarines; and the air was filled with gun smoke, explosions, flames and disaster. Erich had seen so much already in his lifetime that he remained quite calm. The ship's steward brought him a cup of coffee on the bridge during the attack. The steward was a gentleman of color (Erich's description) who was so terrified by the bedlam that " he paled to almost white." The steward, in turn, described Erich to his fellow kitchen crew as follows: *"That old man on the bridge, he pisses ice water!"* When this was repeated to Erich, he was quite tickled at the description. After all that he had seen in his lifetime up to that point, Erich felt little fear of death. He remained calm in the face of danger but he could have a really short fuse in the face of injustice.

The wolf packs were active not just in the North Atlantic, but also along the east coast of the United States and the Norwegian and Barents Seas. But Erich had lived through so much that this was just another challenge. He made the long, bitter cold, run to Murmansk on several occasions. Old snapshots showed the decks and all the stanchions encased in thick ice. Sadly, those photos are of too poor quality to be reproduced. More than one ship was torpedoed in those waters. Any survivors would have died in minutes in the bitter cold waters above the Arctic Circle.

Erich's service with the "Marine Transport Lines" consisted of the following :

SS Swift Arrow	3rd Mate	11/21/40	to	5/9/41
SS Swift Arrow	2nd Mate	5/10/41	to	8/10/41
SS Swift Arrow	2nd Mate	8/29/41	to	10/7/41
SS Swift Arrow	Chief Mate	10/8/41	to	10/25/41
SS Swift Arrow	2nd Mate	10/26/41	to	2/23/42
M/V Panam	Chief Mate	7/15/42	to	3/30/43
SS Richard Olney	Master	3/31/43	to	11/30/43

Although the *Olney* was torpedoed in Sept. 1943, Erich remained with the ship until her cargo was transferred in November.

Chapter 14
Torpedoing of the Richard Olney

On or about September 17th, the *Richard Olney* was berthed in Oran awaiting formations of a convoy to Salerno beachhead. During a blackout, Erich slipped and fell down the ladder from the bridge, cracking several ribs. The following is his account taken from the handwritten report he prepared after the incident.

September 19, 1943(Sunday) at about 8:30 a.m.

Richard Olney passed the breakwater, going out from Oran, bound for Salerno, Italy, with a combat load (T.N.T., ammunition, cordite, aviation gasoline, some stores and vehicles). Passing the breakwater, the degaussing system [14] was put on. In getting up to the convoy the Olney received the #13, which put her last ship in the first column (suicide corner).

September 21st at about 2:30 p.m., a message from the convoy commander was received saying: "Submarine and torpedo track seen on the port side of the convoy." At 8:10 p.m., all ships had to release smoke floats.

At dusk we formed 2 columns and Olney as last ship, received orders to follow in the wake of the preceding ship. It was a dark and cloudy night and Olney had to keep close to the ship ahead, the only one we could see. I was on the bridge all the time. The ship ahead slowed down several times and about 12:15 a.m., started to zigzag.(Erich spells it the German way ...zick zack). I said to the second mate, Mr. Lundy, 'That fellow ahead must have lost contact with the convoy, full ahead on the engine and pass him, I don't want to lose the convoy.' We passed him and soon picked up two ships ahead and three escort vessels. At 1:30 a.m. it cleared up a little and soon the stars came through. I went on the flying bridge and took an azimuth of the North Star to check my compass, and took a bearing of the high land, which became visible by this time. I then told the second mate that we could not go much longer on this course as we would not clear Fratelli Rocks. At this moment the escort vessels started to "??? red flag" (not intelligible) and all ships changed course about 100 degrees to the left. We stayed on this course for about one hour and then went back to our original course. Everything went well now and about 5:30 a.m. I went in my room and sat down on the settee, as I had been on the bridge practically uninterrupted for two days and two nights. I fell asleep but was out again at about 7:30 a.m. Everything was clear, we could see all the convoy; the two ships and we were picking up fast on the convoy. I asked the chief mate what he was steering and how many revolutions the engine was turning. He told me the course had been changed a little while ago and the engine was turning sixty-six revolutions. We were right in the wake of the preceding ship, which was about 400 yards ahead. I went to my room to wash my face and eat breakfast. I looked at the clock as I sat down to eat my breakfast, which was served to me in my office because I had a couple of ribs broken. It was exactly 7:55 a.m. At this instant a terrible explosion occurred and I was thrown up against the ceiling of my office. I was stunned for just a moment, but realizing what had happened, I pushed a typewriter, electric fan and kerosene lamp, which were on top of me, aside and was on the bridge in a moment. Everything was a shamble. As no alarm or whistle worked, I had the signal for "I am torpedoed" hoisted up and ordered the guns fired, first of all to prevent the sub from firing a second torpedo and secondly to attract the attention of the escorts. Having ascertained that the engine was out and I could not fight an outbreak of fire, I had soundings taken to see how the bulkheads held. Lifeboats and life raft lashings were released but I told the crew as well as the soldiers (he was carrying a contingent of troops as well as his cargo), to lay off from the boats, as the ship would not sink and it was our duty to save both the ship and cargo if possible. I ordered all hands forward to get out towing lines. Crew as well as soldiers behaved very well and there was no panic. The rest can be seen in the reports of the crewmembers. Out of 217 men on board, 2 men were lost in the engine room and about 10 were hospitalized, of course practically everyone was badly shaken. I will give just a few instances of the force of the explosion: The main engine was set four feet out of the center of the ship to the port side. On the starboard side the decks were ripped open and pieces of steel had penetrated through three iron decks. A pencil on the desk in my office was blown to matchwood. I had a comb tucked into my hairbrush in my bathroom and when I wanted to use it the next day, I found all the teeth stuck in my hairbrush and disconnected from the comb.

Signed: E. Richter
Formerly in command of the Richard Olney

***

The following are copies of letters written by various members of the crew, describing the torpedoing of the *Richard Olney*. Since the copies of the original letters do not lend themselves to scanning, I have copied each one down as it was written. The first is from Chief Officer, Michael Melnichenko, followed by the report by Barry R. Lundy, 2nd officer, Alvin Carr, 3rd mate, Able Seaman Robert W.Perkins, and a joint statement signed by nine crew members.

***

Vessel   SS. Richard Olney
Port Bizerte, Tunisia
Date September 22,1943

The torpedoing of the SS. Richard Olney as observed by chief Officer, Michael Melnitchenko.

As Chief Officer of the SS. Richard Olney standing the 4 to 8 watch, I relieved the second officer at 3:45 a.m., September 22. I received all information from Mr. Lundy, 2nd Officer, pertaining to position of the vessel and immediately proceeded to check on the present position of the vessel with the second officer going below at 4:10 a.m.

There were two escort vessels aft and one escort vessel forward with the two cargo ships ahead. I maintained proper position until time of explosion by obtaining continuous bearings and adjusting engine speed accordingly. Approximately twenty minutes prior to the torpedoing of the ship, the naval signalman presented me with a message from the escort vessel to follow directly in the wake of the proceeding vessel. Upon receipt of this message I promptly instructed the wheelman to carry out this instruction. This order having been carried out, I was on the port wing of the bridge observing the position of the vessel, when the explosion occurred on the starboard side at 7:55 a.m. I immediately attempted to sound the whistle signal, which I found to be out of order. I requested from the wheelman as to whether or not she had steerage. At this time the Captain entered the pilothouse and threw in the General Alarm, which was also out of order. He then instructed A.B.Perkins to run up the appropriate signal for "I have been torpedoed" This having been done the Captain took command of the vessel and ordered me to check on damage. After I reported on the damage the Captain stated he was of the opinion the vessel would not sink so he instructed us to take the crew forward and make preparations for being towed.

*Signed: Michael Melnitchenko,
Chief Officer*

***

The following is the report of Barry R. Lundy, the Second Officer of the *Richard Olney*.

***

To whom it may concern;

I, Barry R. Lundy, 2nd Officer of the SS. Richard Olney, make the following statement relative to the torpedoing of the ship off Bizerte, Tunisia, on September 22, 1945 and the conduct of the entire personnel aboard at that time. Being 2nd Officer, my watch was the 12 to 4 and being relieved at 0400 September 22, 1945, by chief Officer Mr. Melnitchenko, I turned over to him all orders and such information as would be helpful to an officer just coming on watch. As is customary, the Chief Officer came on the bridge about 0345 and I remained with him while his eyes were becoming adjusted to the darkness. Captain Richter was on the bridge with us at the time as he was unable to sleep because of broken ribs suffered in a fall in Oran during a blackout.

Captain Richter left the bridge with me and we went to the chart room to check the position and course on the chart. From there he returned to the bridge and I went below, turning in about 0500.

I was suddenly awakened, by a terrific explosion, that threw me out of my bunk and onto my chair. I was on my feet instantly and surmising what had happened, my only thoughts were to get the lifeboats in the water if the ship was sinking and try to rescue everyone possible, or if the ship remained afloat, to care for the injured.

As I jerked open the door to my room, smoke and steam poured in and, as I made my way through it to the boat deck, I realized that the whistle and general alarm must either be out of commission or the watch on the bridge had been knocked out. I didn't know whether the Captain and the Chief Officer were alive.

On reaching the boat deck I saw the ship was righting herself and steadying up and some of the crewmembers were arriving. I ordered boat grips released but to await further orders before lowering. At this same instant I heard Captain Richter giving orders from the bridge. Even before the men could obey my order, he gave the same order to me. He also ordered all guns fired to attract attention as the whistle had no steam, and to raise the signal for "I have been torpedoed." He then ordered the fire hoses laid out fore and aft but finding no pumps working, he ordered the men to let the hoses go and stand by to assist wherever needed.

Seeing the Chief Officer and the 3rd Officer were on the bridge to assist the Captain, I immediately went to the main deck starboard side of number 3 hatch to check off the crew and ascertain if any were missing. I asked Lt. Oakes to check the soldiers and Mr. Seaman, Gunnery Officer, for a report on his men. All the gun crew were accounted for with none injured and all the soldiers were accounted for with a few minor injuries; but as the ship's crew checked off, several injured men staggered up and I got them on cots and called for assistance. More men responded than could be used. Soldiers as well as crewmen came and were ready to do whatever they could. Among these were the Army Officers and Medical Corps Corporal and the ship's steward and a utility man, Fitts. I had been told that Fitts was once an Army Medical Officer and in this emergency he proved very valuable and must be commended. He had suffered a head injury himself but didn't let that stop him. Also I wish to commend the Army Officer and the Medical Corps Corporal and the ship's 3rd Assistant Engineer for the aid rendered the injured.

My check of the crew revealed that two men were missing, Luke, an oiler, and Malcolm, a fireman. I was told that they were below on watch and trapped by the explosion and it would be impossible to get to them. This was the first idea of what time the torpedo hit. I then learned that it had hit at about 7:55 a.m. It was then 0810 and as I worked with the injured men the Captain called on everyone, soldiers as well as crew members, to give a hand wherever needed.

The injured crew members according to degree of injury were:

Robert Birdsey	Purser –severe
Edward Wilson	2nd cook –severe
Jean R. Trombley	2nd cook-severe
Robert D. Walker	Utility – severe
Leonard J. Langdon	1st asst Eng.
Nathan P. Fitts	Utility

James E. Gray	*Messman*
Jesse T.Liles	*Ordinary seaman*
Wilhelm W. Maki	*Chief cook*

At about 0840, a small British escort came to take us in tow. At 0900 a British escort came up and passed us a towline and sent their doctor aboard. On both occasions Captain Richter called on the soldiers to assist our crew in handling lines and they responded. At 10:30 a tug arrived from Bizerte and relieved the escort vessel and again, the soldiers pitched in to help handle the lines.

When we came to anchor at 12:15, boats began to arrive from shore bringing a U.S.Army doctor and we began disembarking the injured at 11:00. Captain Richter deserves high commendation for the handling of this emergency and so do all the members of the crew for the way they kept their heads and promptly carried out his orders. The Army personnel are due commendation for their assistance.

It was not until after we came to anchor that I had an opportunity to properly survey the damage done, and satisfy myself that it was caused by a torpedo. After having inspected everything I was convinced it was a torpedo that struck the ship. This conclusion has since been substantiated by British Officers of the tug that has been furnishing steam.

They have been doing salvage work since the war began and have seen ships that were torpedoed and others that hit mines and they say they will stake their reputation that we were torpedoed.

Barry R. Lundy,
Second Officer

***

Joint statement of the torpedoing of the *SS. Richard Olney* by ship's crew.
(Phraseology and punctuation is as originally written!)

***

We, the undersigned members of the crew of the SS. Richard Olney, having been engaged in our duties or either in our forecastle at the time of the explosion, are unable to state anything definite but the majority of us are of the opinion the explosion was due to a torpedo.

As those of us who were awake and had been on deck prior to the explosion had observed that we were the last in the column with two ships directly ahead. In our opinion had it been anything other than a torpedo it would possibly have struck one of the two ships ahead. or have struck us elsewhere instead of on the starboard side and going through into the engine room. The concussion was centered mid-ship with a hole blown through the starboard side with the plates buckling on the port side. No.3 and No.5 lifeboats, which were directly over the hole made by the explosion, were completely undamaged as well as the upper portion of the hull in the area of contacting the torpedo.

Signed by:
Vincent Stasellman   *Elijah T. Hall*
Robert E. Russell   *George Stanley Ichton*
Jose Pirez   *John Kotter*
Nils E. Kuustinen (sp. Illegible)
Lester G. Amsinger   *David R. Tuck*

***

Statement by Alvin W. Carr, 3rd Mate of the SS Richard Olney

***

At 7:55 a.m. September 22. as I was ready to go on watch, the ship was struck by a torpedo. I immediately went to the hurricane deck to assist the captain. We had given orders to loose the grips on the lifeboats and had them ready for lowering. We gave the order to fire the

ships guns all around the ship to keep the submarine from firing another torpedo at us.

As soon as a destroyer came near, the Captain requested them to send a doctor aboard to treat the injured, which they did as soon as they had us in tow.

I wish to compliment the Army, Navy and Merchantmen and Officers for their behavior at this time, especially the Captain who did all possible to save the lives of us all, also saved the ship.

Signed: Alvin W. Carr, 3rd Mate

***

Statement of the torpedoing of the *SS. Richard Olney* as observed by Able Seaman, Robert S. Perkins:

Having been at the wheel at the time of the explosion, in all probability I had the best opportunity of observing the incidents immediately following. Because of this, I was asked by the Captain to write a statement of the incident as observed by me.

The explosion occurred at 7:55 a.m. September 22, 1943. The ship having been struck on the starboard side by, what was believed to have been, a torpedo exploding into the engine room, causing the death of the oiler and fireman on watch and wounding ten men, of which two or three were severely injured.

Approximately twenty minutes prior to the torpedoing a message was delivered to the chief Officer by the Naval signalman with instructions to follow the wake of the preceding vessel; this order having been immediately executed there was nothing unusual happening until the time of the explosion.

As a result of the explosion the steering apparatus was completely out of operation. The chief Officer attempted to sound the signal whistle but all possible means of sound communications were out of order, also the blinker system was temporarily out of order

By this time the Captain was on the bridge and gave orders to run up the appropriate signal for having been torpedoed and for all hands to clear away lifeboats but not to lower until proper orders, and the carpenter was ordered to take some soundings.

The Gunnery Officer opened fire with guns immediately after the explosion, for the purpose of scaring off subs and attracting the attention of the escort and shore stations.

The wounded were placed on number three hatch, and first aid treatment was administered by 2nd Officer Mr. Lundy, A.B.Russell and Utility man N. Fitts, and enough praise cannot be given the work these men did.

At nine a.m. a towing line was taken aboard and the ship proceeded underway by tow, the Doctor having been sent aboard immediately after the towing cable was made fast. The behavior of the Merchant crew, Naval gun crew and soldiers was superb and, with the exception of momentary confusion following the explosion, all orders were carried out with harmonious efficiency. The ship anchored inside the break-water at Bizerte at 12:15 p.m.

Signed: Robert M. Perkins

***

This concludes the written reports by the crew members of the "*Richard Olney*"

Erich stayed aboard the ship with a skeleton crew while the cargo was transferred to the *John Fisk*. The following was a P.S. on Erich's report:

"On October 5th the cargo was completely transferred to the Fisk and on October 6th the Olney was beached in Bizerte Lake in nineteen feet of water, where she will be for the duration."

Since wartime security demanded secrecy, Erich's family knew nothing of the torpedoing for some time. Kate received phone calls, first from the 3rd Officer and then the 2nd Officer, just telling her that the Captain was fine and would be home soon. A few weeks later there was another spate of calls from the engineers of the *Olney*— all with the same message --- *"The Captain is fine and will be home soon."* Kate was puzzled but didn't have a clue as to what was keeping Erich away while all his officers were coming home. With the war still raging, all information regarding shipping and military activities were still "secret," but by November, Kate's patience had run out. She marched into the office of the "Marine Transport Company" and demanded an explanation! It just so happened that this was the day preceding Erich's return to New York as temporary Master of the *William Webb* so Kate was given the details of all that had transpired.

Most of what I learned from my father about the entire incident was played down as normal. Now that I have copies of documents I have finally learned the details of the entire *Olney* incident. The following pages contain copies of letters from the War Shipping Administration. Wherever possible I have scanned the original letters and inserted them into the text. In some cases the documents I have are carbon copies on onionskin and scanning did not produce legible copies. In those cases I copied the letters exactly, including phraseology and punctuation (or lack thereof.)

***

Bizerte, Tunisia

November 20, 1943
Marine Transport Lines, Inc.
11 Broadway
New York, New York

Attention: Mr. H. J. Muuss, Operating Manager, Cargo Division
Dear Sir:

S.S. Richard Olney

We duly received your letter of November 4, 1943 and pleased to learn that a copy of our letter of October 7th addressed to our Regional Headquarters at Algiers had reached you together with enclosures giving report on damage of above vessel by explosion from torpedo or mine off Tunisian coast and statements covering status of crew members as of said date.

We trust that you will also have received copy of our supplementary report to Algiers dated October 25th with enclosures forwarded therewith which would enable you to deal with all matters pertaining to members of the ship's crew repatriated subsequent to our above mentioned letter of October 7th.

As regards the question of repairs to the Richard Olney, you will no doubt have received advices from the War Shipping Administration in Washington concerning plans under consideration for dealing with their several vessels presently tied up in this area awaiting opportunity for drydocking and carrying out of necessary repairs. We would only add in this connection that the damage suffered by the Olney as far as can be judged without dry-docking of vessel appears to be of such an extensive and serious nature that arrangements are being made to place a small French standby crew on board as caretakers in order to release Captain Richter and all remaining members of his crew for return to the States. It is now expected that steamer will remain tied up in her present anchorage in Lake Bizerte for considerable time, probably until the close of the war owing to difficulty of securing dry-dock for effecting repairs at this port.

We wish to take this opportunity of stating that Captain Richter has cooperated with this office to the fullest extent in dealing with all problems arising in connection with the handling of vessel following arrival at Bizerte after the explosion occurred September 22, 1943 and the salvage of the ship's entire cargo which was transferred to the SS John Fisk and forwarded on to its final destination, as well as the safeguarding and preservation of all ship's equipment and furnishings remaining intact after the explosion, has been due largely to his constant watchfulness and devotion to duty in protecting in every possible manner the interest of owners entrusted to his care.

Yours very truly,

Signed,   M.L.Glidewell, Port Representative,
*   War Shipping Administration*
cc: WSA, Algiers
be: Capt. Richter, SS Richard Olney

***

UNITED STATES OF AMERICA
WAR   SHIPPING   ADMINISTRATION

Bizerte, Tunisia

November 21, 1943
Capt. Erich Richter
SS Richard Olney
Bizerte, Tunisia
Dear Captain,

We beg to confirm verbal advices furnished you to effect that arrangements have been concluded in accordance with telephonic for appointment of Captain Georges LeFlohic as Master of the SS Richard Olney with standby crew of four (4) French seamen, to assume charge of vessel, together with all equipment, furnishings and stores on board., effective as from noon this date, thus enabling you to proceed to Algiers to take command of another Liberty ship presently at that port.

The present will also serve to confirm arrangements made for you to travel by Military air transport service from Bizerte to Algiers and we enclose herewith Special Orders No. 260 issued by Headquarters, Eastern Base Section, dated November 20, 1943, authorizing such travel. In this connection we would add that reservation for space has been made on first plane leaving from local airport early tomorrow morning for Algiers which also includes extra baggage allowance up to 200 pounds and we have advised our office in Algiers of your expected departure accordingly. Incidentally, we would mention that the remaining four (4) members of your crew who have been serving as members of stand-by crew on the Olney are being repatriated per the SS John Rutledge scheduled to sail from this port for the States with next GUS convoy.

Yours very truly,

M. L. Glidewell
Port Representative
War Shipping Administration
cc:WBA, Algiers

***

Algiers, Algeria

December 6, 1943
Mr. G. H. Helmbold

War Shipping Administration,
WASHINGTON, D.C.
Subject-. Captain E. Richter.

Dear Sir,

Since the commencement of Operations in this area there have been some outstanding Masters. Among these I wish to mention Captain E. Richter, formerly Master of the Steamer Richard Olney.

The Richard Olney was badly damaged by enemy action in the Mediterranean. Captain Richter, by his excellent seamanship, strength of character and general ability, kept his crew under control and brought his ship into port at Bizerte. Since that time he has stood by her with a skeleton crew under very unpleasant conditions. Needing a Master for a vessel due to return to the United States, Captain Richter was approached and willingly volunteered.

I wish to bring the above to your attention and feel that Captain Richter is deserving of special mention for excellence in the performance of his duties.

Yours very truly
(Sgd.) C.W.Kalloch Regional Director, N.A.
War Shipping Administration

***

After the torpedoing of the *Richard Olney*, Erich quickly resumed his duties. He brought the *William H. Webb* home from Africa, and had the option of remaining her captain but declined. A different shipping company was in charge of the *Webb*, and Erich had been very satisfied with the Marine Transport Line. Therefore he chose to remain in their employ. Two of the officers from the *Webb* liked serving with Erich and joined him on his next assignment, the *James B. Aswell*, on February 16, 1944. The *Webb* headed for Murmansk and was lost, "all hands," another close call for Erich.

Chapter 15
Commission

The United States Maritime Service had been established to lend dignity to a service that was providing such valuable help to our war effort. Merchant mariners, in the past, had been looked down on as something less than their fellow seafarers in the Navy, although they were just as exposed to danger. On March 10,1944, Erich applied for a commission in the newly formed Service. A copy of both front and back pages of his application follows.

***

MISSISSIPPI SHIPPING COMPANY, INC.
NEW ORLEANS, LA.

SERVICE RECORD

New Orleans
(PLACE)
March 10th 1944
(DATE)

Name in full *Erich Richter*

Permanent home address *104 Wakeman Place* Phone *Shore Road 5-230* *Brooklyn N.Y.*

Born—Town *Ransfelde* State *Prussia* Country *Germany*

Month *August* Day *14th* Year *1882*

Naturalized at *Brooklyn N.Y.* Date *Jan. 7th 1936*

Height *5' 10"* Married or single *Married*

What certificate do you now hold? *Master*

Date of certificate *Feb. 26th 1941* License and issue numbers *2 - 2*

(Hold Master Steam & Sail, March 28th 1908)

Where issued *New York*

Has such certificate ever been suspended? *No*

Where received training and education not shown under particulars of sea service?

Cause of vacating last position

(Signature) *C. Richter*

Position Desired

Assigned to S. S. _____ Date _____

Transferred }
Resigned } _____ Date _____
Relieved }

(SEE OTHER SIDE FOR PARTICULARS OF SEA SERVICE)
Application will not be considered unless record is given in full and date of entering and leaving each position is accurately shown.

Any false statement made will subject applicant to dismissal from employment.

FORM 813—5M—111943

Application for Commission

PARTICULARS OF SEA SERVICE

VESSEL	SIZE	TYPE	RATING	FROM—	TO—	OWNER

Served on square riggers from April 1896 to 1906 10½ years—last trip to Mattem on a Fourmast Barque

From 1906 to 1914 of Hansa Line 3rd, 2nd to Chief Mate — (10.000 Ton ships Run around the world)

Served as Master on "Concho" "Amulgee" "Kish" "Marisal Suire" "Goyaaz" "Mosquera" "Matay" "Panam"

Since March 1943 Master on "Richard Olney" to November 21, 1943 (torpedoed)

November 22th to December 18th "William H. Webb" Master

Assigned to "Jas B. Cawell" Master

Febrito

To be inserted after each vessel:
Column "Size"—Deck officers, tonnage; engineer officers, horsepower.
Column "Type"—Deck officers, steam, sail, or auxiliary; engineer officers, reciprocating, turbine, or Diesel.

On March 21, 1944 Erich received his Commission as Commander in the United States Maritime Service.

WAR SHIPPING ADMINISTRATION TRAINING ORGANIZATION

MS 7
(January 1943)

United States **Maritime Service**

Designation of Grade

This is to certify that

ERICH RICHTER   (4430-02499)

has this date been designated

Commander (D)

in the UNITED STATES MARITIME SERVICE

Effective _____ March 21 _____, 19 44

~~Originaxxxx~~xxxx _____ *on* _____
                    (Place)   (Date)

~~Exploxxxxxx~~xxx _____ *on* _____
                    (Place)   (Date)

Date of issue ___ March 21 ___ 19 44

(Signature of enrollee)

L. G. LIVINGSTON
Lieutenant Commander, U.S.M.S.
Personnel Officer

Commission

The following letter accompanied the official appointment stressing pride in the Service:

"The commission which you have just obtained represents far more than the right to wear the uniform and distinctive insignia of the United States Maritime Service. It affords you and your fellow officers an opportunity to create an officers corps that can well take its place besides those of other services.

For the first time in the long history of the United States Merchant Marine, a Federal body is lending its efforts to the task of securing for merchant marine officers the recognition, respect and reward which they so richly deserve. Recognition and respect are not to be had for the asking-they must be earned and the task involved is not an easy one.

The success or failure of this effort depends squarely upon you as an individual. Gold braid does not make an officer; knowledge, skill, bearing a proper mental attitude and conduct do.

An officer, who by his actions, brings criticism upon himself brings criticism on the organization of which he is a part. Such actions make the task of a young organization striving for recognition doubly difficult. The wholehearted cooperation of each individual wearing the uniform of the United States Merchant Service, his exemplary conduct and the feeling in himself that he is an officer worthy of the name will make our task a more simple one. Given the honest effort of every officer we can together win a prestige born of dignity, principle and high purpose."

At last, the American Merchant Mariners received recognition and respect and a uniform to wear with pride and dignity. They were no longer looked down on as less valuable than members of the other military services and they laid their lives on the line along with the bravest.

Commander Erich Richter 1944

Chapter 16
Move to the Country

Life resumed a peaceful happy course. With all the family grown, Kate was free to travel to any port where Erich might anchor. They lived the good life…fine restaurants in every port and accommodations at the best hotels; they even began to think seriously of buying a home.

In 1944, Kate had traveled to a small town in Connecticut to visit Erich Jr, and to see his daughter, her newest grandchild. She fell in love with the quiet village. Since I was alone with a new baby while my husband Hugh was overseas with the 8th Army, I had moved back home. During her visit to Connecticut, Kate found a house for rent that was large enough to accommodate us. With Erich's consent and Hugh's approval, Kate and I, along with my infant son, packed up bag and baggage and moved to "the country."

On a visit home, Erich and Kate took long walks enjoying the rural surroundings. Since they had both come from small towns, this was like a long overdue homecoming. But the war continued, supplies were needed on both fronts, and Erich's brief visit home soon came to an end.

Erich went back to work and really thought nothing further about the complimentary remarks made about his handling of the *Olney* torpedoing. He was assigned to the *James B. Aswell* on February 16, 1944, and continued delivering the valuable war cargos to our troops in Europe and the Pacific. With the cessation of hostilities in Europe on May 7, 1945, the Atlantic Ocean became a little safer, although there was still a problem of floating mines. Fortunately, Erich had no further problems with explosions. After his early experiences aboard the *Nimrod* in 1903, and the

143

torpedoing of the *Richard Olney* in 1943, he had already had his fair share of "fireworks."

The day of the Japanese surrender (VJ Day), August 14, 1945, all enemy action ceased, and the U-boats finally were no longer a threat.

At some point before September 21, 1946, Erich had been assigned as Master of yet another ship, the *SS Martha Berry*. On that date he made a trip to his old "home port" of Bremen. Security was still tight and the "Counter Intelligence Corps" was in charge of security as evidenced by the information on the security pass issued to him.

***

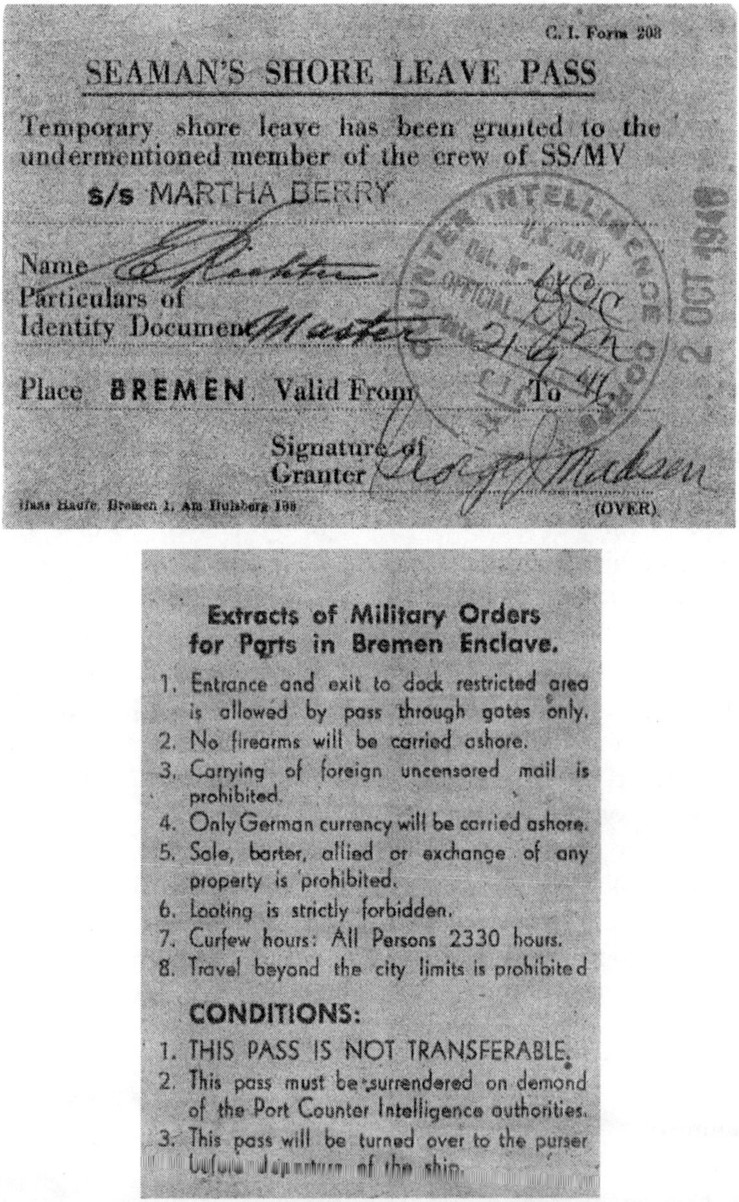

C. I. Form 208

SEAMAN'S SHORE LEAVE PASS

Temporary shore leave has been granted to the undermentioned member of the crew of SS/MV

s/s MARTHA BERRY

Name

Particulars of Identity Document

Place BREMEN Valid From To

Signature of Granter

Hans Haufe, Bremen 1, Am Hulsberg 138 (OVER)

COUNTER INTELLIGENCE CORPS U.S. ARMY OFFICIAL

2 OCT 1946

Extracts of Military Orders for Ports in Bremen Enclave.

1. Entrance and exit to dock restricted area is allowed by pass through gates only.
2. No firearms will be carried ashore.
3. Carrying of foreign uncensored mail is prohibited.
4. Only German currency will be carried ashore.
5. Sale, barter, allied or exchange of any property is prohibited.
6. Looting is strictly forbidden.
7. Curfew hours: All Persons 2330 hours.
8. Travel beyond the city limits is prohibited

CONDITIONS:

1. THIS PASS IS NOT TRANSFERABLE.
2. This pass must be surrendered on demand of the Port Counter Intelligence authorities.
3. This pass will be turned over to the purser before departure of the ship.

Shore leave pass for Bremen

It was certainly a different return to Bremen for him…no longer the boy that first embraced the life of a seafarer so long ago in 1898. So much had happened since his last sailing from Bremen. Although Erich was a dedicated American citizen and proud of his service, there most have been a few nostalgic moments. This was the country of his birth; this was the city that had been home so long ago, where his daughter and son were born. He did meet some old friends, among them a man named Anton Seidenzahl and his wife. Anton had been Erich's Chief Mate on the *Mariscal Sucre* in Colombia, and when that war ended, the Seidenzahls, who were not US citizens, had returned to Germany. Erich was happy to see them once more because he and Anton had become good friends.

The torpedoing of the *Richard Olney* was history and, except to stay in touch with some of the survivors, Erich got on with his life. Now the freight ships were kept busy carrying material to rebuild Europe and, in some cases, to ferry prisoners of war home.

He was appointed Master of a brand new Victory class ship, *Adelphi Victory,* and dispatched to the Sea of Japan. His duties included supervising the removal of gun emplacements on the freight ships that would be transporting former prisoners of war.

In late December of 1945 he became aware of a swelling below his left ear. When it became apparent that the swelling wouldn't just recede, he went aboard the hospital ship *USS Bountiful* on January 22 1946. The report of the medical staff aboard the *Bountiful* follows herewith:

***

U.S.S.BOUNTIFUL (AH-9)

January 22, 1946

Certificate of Treatment was issued:
Name of Patient: Erich Richter
Rank of Patient: Captain USMS
Date admitted to this command: 20 January, 1946
Diagnosis upon Admission: Undetermined Tumor on Neck.
Chief Complaint: Lumps on left side of face.

History of present illness: 6 weeks before admission to this command, patient noticed a swelling behind and below the left ear. Has had no pain, but swelling has had a tendency to increase gradually in size and appears to be extending on to the face in front of the ear. He describes a slight discomfort on the anterior border of the Trapazine [15] at its insertion on the scapula. Also has a history of diabetes.

Physical Examination: Essentially negative except for a tumor in the region of the left parotid gland. The swelling is about plum size, apparently fixed, non tender and not particularly hard. It has none of the characteristics of a mixed tumor of the parotid except for its location.

1-22-46: Laboratory reports a blood sugar of 200, urea N 15 and urea 31 mgm. X-Rays of chest negative. X-Ray of mandible and maxilla show no body abnormality or other cause of the underlying pathology. In view of the nature of the pathology it is advisable for him to be returned to the U.S.A. by air at the earliest possible date for further diagnostic procedures. It is my opinion that a biopsy should not be performed on this ship as facilities for the radical procedure necessary in the event a malignancy is found are inadequate.

Discharged this date.

(signed) O.F.SMITH
Lt.Comdt MC USNR

APPROVED:(signed) L.W. Johnson

LEWIS W. JOHNSON, CAPTAIN MC US
CERTIFIED TRUE COPY(sgnd)
SENIOR MEDICAL OFFICER
E. Richter, Master, SS ADELPHI VICTOR

Chapter 17
The Medal

In February Erich flew home to Connecticut and consulted with the family physician, Doctor W.B. Walker. He was admitted into the local hospital and a biopsy of the tumor was taken. The consensus of the pathologist and other consulting physicians was that the tumor was benign. In March, plans were made for him to return to duty when he received the following;

WAR SHIPPING ADMINISTRATION
WASHINGTON

March 21, 1946
Captain Erich Richter
West Cornwall, Connecticut

Dear Captain Richter:

We are anxious to get in touch with you regarding your actions aboard the SS Richard Olney. It is requested that you wire this office collect upon your next return to the United States, giving us your present address.

We would also like to know how long you plan to be ashore.

Sincerely yours,
Frank Rusk
Executive Secretary
Merchant Marine Decorations and Medals Board

***

Erich was astounded and quick to reply to Mr. Rusk's letter since a second letter from Mr. Rusk acknowledges receipt of reply from Erich.

WAR SHIPPING ADMINISTRATION
WASHINGTON Zone 25
March 26, 1946
SPECIAL DELIVERY

Captain Erich Richter
Box 20
West Cornwall, Connecticut

Dear Captain Richter;

This will acknowledge receipt of your telegram of March 23. We are pleased to inform you that you have been awarded the Merchant Marine Meritorious Service Medal for your services while Master of the SS Richard Olney. From your telegram, we assume that you will ship out again around the first of April. If this is true, it is requested that you wire us collect the port from which you will ship and the date that you will arrive at this part, in order that we may arrange for formal presentation of the medal to you.

Inasmuch as the policy governing the award of this medal requires that it be presented by a high-ranking official of the Maritime Commission or War Shipping Administration with an appropriate ceremony, it will be appreciated if you will let us have the above information as far in advance as possible, so that we have sufficient time to arrange for the presentation. It is urgently requested that you keep the fact that you have been awarded a medal CONFIDENTIAL as it is the policy of the Merchant Marine Decorations and Medals Board not to inform a recipient of an award until the day of the presentation. We also want to avoid premature publicity.

Sincerely yours
Frank Rusk, Executive Secretary
Merchant Marine Decorations and Medals Board

***

It is difficult to imagine what Erich must have felt upon receiving this notice. His whole life had been devoted to performing his duties with honor and dignity, and yet his character had been questioned, he had been removed from his ship at gunpoint and had been investigated by not only the Naval Intelligence but also by the F.B.I. Here, finally, was vindication and respect and honor.

***

A copy of the citation is on the following page.

WAR SHIPPING ADMINISTRATION
WASHINGTON, D. C.

OFFICE OF THE ADMINISTRATOR

The ADMINISTRATOR, WAR SHIPPING ADMINISTRATION, takes pleasure in commending

ERICH RICHTER, MASTER

for MERITORIOUS SERVICE as set forth in the following

CITATION:

In September 1943, SS RICHARD OLNEY, under the command of Captain Richter, was torpedoed off the north coast of Africa. A large hole was torn in the vessel's side, the boilers and engineroom were wrecked and machinery plant rendered useless. Despite three fractured ribs suffered only two days before, the Master took immediate charge of the ship and crew, and by his fine example and personal leadership allayed any tendency to panic. Temporary repairs were effected and every possible step taken to keep the ship afloat. In response to a request for assistance a Naval escort vessel came alongside, took a hawser from the damaged ship and towed her to a North African port. The RICHARD OLNEY was then beached in a protected location and her vital military cargo was successfully discharged. Captain Richter's cool and courageous bearing, his expert seamanship and his ability as a commander of men contributed greatly to this fortunate result and will be a lasting inspiration to seamen of the United States Merchant Marine.

A copy of this commendation for MERITORIOUS SERVICE has been made a part of Captain Richter's official record.

Emory Scott Land,

Emory Scott Land
Administrator

December 11, 1945

Citation

The Merchant Marine Meritorious Service Medal

Medal

Erich's ribbons, in addition to the Merchant Marine Meritorious Service Medal, include the Philippine Liberation Ribbon, Atlantic War Zone Bar, The Merchant Marine Defense Bar, the Pacific War Zone Bar, The Merchant

Defense Bar, the Pacific War Zone Bar, The Merchant Marine Combat Bar and the Mediterranean Middle East War Zone Bar.

The following photo was taken at the presentation.

Erich receiving his medal on March 26, 1946
The swelling behind his left ear is clearly visible.

The citation accompanying the medal was actually issued on December 11, 1945. Arranging for the presentation took some time because it had to be presented in the United states and Erich was out of the country until his sudden trip home for medical reasons. He returned to sea, but in May he was again in consultation with Doctor Walker. It is impossible to scan the original, so I have copied it verbatim.

***

W. BRADFORD WALKER, M.D.
Cornwall, Conn.

May 21, 1946

TO WHOM IT MAY CONCERN

Capt. Erich Richter of West Cornwall, has been under our care and observation off and on since early in February when he returned from Japan with a large swelling on the left side of the neck. After surgical and radiological consultation, he was hospitalized for biopsy. This was done and there was some difference of opinion among several pathologists as to etiology of the swelling. Frank pus was encountered on the incision, which grew only a staphylococcus on culture.

A second biopsy was done later and at that time pus was again encountered and following excision of the tissue this time penicillin was given for several days without appreciable difference in the size of the gland.

It has been the opinion of our pathologist and four others who have inspected the tissue that it is chronic inflammatory tissue and there is no evidence of malignancy.

Following this, on the advice of the surgeon, he was given a course of Iodine again without any appreciable difference in the gland. He recently had three remaining bad teeth extracted after which there was an abscess in the jaw, and the swelling in the gland which is on the other side became considerably worse. This now appears to be subsiding and his general condition remains good.

He is anxious to return to sea and I see no reason why he should not be allowed to make short trips, if he is not too many weeks away from medical aid in case the gland should break down and require drainage.

Any further inquiries regarding Capt. Richter's condition can be addressed to me or to Dr. Thomas J. Danaher, 106 Litchfield Street, Torrington, Connecticut, who is the consulting surgeon.

(SGD) W.BRADFORD WALKER, M.D

Handwritten on the bottom of this letter Erich has entered the following:

From June 3rd to June 15th received 12 more injections of Penicillin (1 daily) of 300,000 units each, making a total of 3,600,000 units in this treatment.

Chapter 18
Diagnosis

During autumn of 1946, Erich and Kate finally found their dream house and made a deposit Erich was still dealing with the swelling behind his left ear and the decision was made for him to enter the Merchant Marine hospital in Baltimore, Maryland. A Radon treatment was begun; this consisted of the implanting of Radon pellets into the site of the swelling.

Erich appeared to be responding well and sounded cheerful and encouraged when Kate spoke with him via telephone. He was looking forward to coming home for a visit at Christmas. I had two children at the time, two-year old boy, Patrick, and an infant daughter, Kathleen. Patrick was the apple of Erich's eye and he looked forward to spending time with him. He arrived home the week before Christmas looking hale and hearty except for an area, behind his ear, that looked sunburned.

Christmas was spent with us in Connecticut and right after Christmas Erich and Kate headed for New York City to spend the rest of the holiday with my sister Olga and her husband. After a big holiday dinner, Erich became ill with an upset stomach. The heavy meal was blamed and he headed back to Baltimore. One week later Erich spoke with Kate again and mentioned that he had had a case of food poisoning. Then word came that he was being discharged and would be home on Saturday, January 18th. We all heaved a sigh of relief. He was coming home; he must be better.

On Saturdays an afternoon train referred to as the "banker's special" arrived in the early afternoon and Kate was there to meet the train. When Erich appeared she almost fainted from the shock. He had become a shadow of his former self in just three weeks. He was so ill that he needed to be helped from the train. The conductor told Kate that they had tried to send him to the hospital in Danbury because he was in such pain, but Erich was determined to come home. Although they lived just around the corner from the station, a neighbor brought a car to take him home. Doctor Walker was summoned and he wanted to take Erich right back to the hospital but nothing would do for Erich but to sleep in his own bed. Because he was too weak to walk up the stairs, his bed was brought down into the living room. He did agree to let the doctor take him to the hospital in the morning.

Sunday morning he was taken to the hospital, burning with fever. The surgeon was contacted to see him on Monday morning. Unfortunately, there was no private room available so Erich was placed in a ten-bed ward.

During all his years at sea he had picked up some pretty salty expressions, and although always a gentleman in mixed company, that didn't count in his delirium. With a temperature of 105 he regaled the entire ward, and all the visitors during visiting hours, with some pretty wild rantings, much to Kate's embarrassment.

By Monday morning a private room became available and the surgeon took over. When Kate went in to hear the outcome she was told that Erich had peritonitis and was beyond saving. However, if he had survived the peritonitis he would have had a longer and more painful journey ahead. He was full of cancer. Two tumors in his small intestines had closed off the track leading to a rupture of the intestine (the cause of his great agony on the train). Since this had occurred on Saturday the peritonitis had a firm hold.

Erich spent the remainder of Monday and the entire night in a state of delirium. The family gathered and we stood vigil. On a few rare occasions, Erich would have a lucid moment. During one such moment he looked at me and recognized me and commented, *"Now I will never see my Paddy again."* He was referring to my son Patrick.

Erich was reliving a great deal of his life in this feverish state. At one point he was calling for a pilot to come aboard in New York harbor. At another time he was on the bridge during a wild storm and spoke about sails. He hadn't been on a sailing ship in over thirty-five years.

We spent the night but left in the early morning to relieve our baby sitter so that she could go to school. We made arrangements to go back to the hospital right after lunch and at 11:30 a.m. the call came. Erich's mighty heart had stopped beating. It was January 21, 1947.

We had a service at the funeral home and with the ground frozen, Erich's body was consigned to a vault until spring. I remember very little about the funeral; I was too numb to cry. I do remember that the minister read a poem by Alfred Lord Tennyson entitled *Crossing the Bar*. I can't think of anything more fitting:

***

Sunset and evening star,
And one clear call for me!
And may there be no moaning of the bar,
When I put out to sea,

But such a tide as moving seems asleep,
Too full for sound and foam,
When that which drew from out the boundless deep
Turns again home.
Twilight and evening bell
And after that the dark
And may there be no sadness of farewell,
When I embark;

For tho' from out our bourne of Time and Place
The flood may bear me far,
I hope to see my Pilot face to face
When I have crossed the bar.

***

After his death, when Kate was going through the belongings in Erich's suitcase, she found a small diary he had kept. On one page in early January there was just one word written and underlined "Melanoma." The large wart that Erich had on top of his left hand, and which he, and everyone else, passed off as "just a wart," was evidently the first sign of future trouble. At the onset of his illness, no one suspected any connection with the wart. Today most of us are far more aware of cancer symptoms. By the time Erich's cancer was finally diagnosed he was already dying.

In the spring of 1947 Erich was laid to rest in the Cornwall, Connecticut cemetery. July 3, 1981, his beloved Kate finally joined him. She had celebrated her 94th birthday just eight days earlier.

Final Rest

ENDNOTES

HOME IS THE SAILOR, HOME FROM THE SEA

1. In German the formal address for you is "Sie" and the familiar is "Du". Apparently Karl was addressing the Captain as Du, a decided lack of respect and a breach of manners.

2. First crossers - a traditional initiation for those crossing the equator for the first time on a ship.

3. Saltpeter was an export of Chile; its coast was called the "saltpeter coast".

4. The bridge to which he refers has to be the Brooklyn Bridge that was completed in 1883.

5. Southwester: a waterproof hat of oilskin and canvas, etc. with broad brim in back to protect the neck; worn in stormy weather.

6. Grossbrass was an extra long, heavy line (hawser) attached to the Mainsail and used to change the mainsail direction. Because of its length and heft it was used whenever a man went overboard, in the hope that the unfortunate would be able to grasp it.

7. Coke is a solid carbonaceous fuel obtained by distilling the volatile constituents from coal by heating in ovens or retorts.

8. Saltpeter's commercial importance is as a fertilizer, in manufacturing of glass, as a food preservative, and in some medications as a diuretic. It was once used in gunpowder and is now found in explosives, fireworks and matches. Reference: *Encarta*

9. Belaying pin: a moveable pin of wood or metal to which running gear may be made fast.

10. Taler: a coin worth 3 Marks.

11. Kaetchen: diminutive form of Kate.

12. Larboard: left. Starboard: right.

13. Wolf Packs were groups of German submarines that would attack Allied convoys from several different directions at the same time...much as wolves circle their prey.

14. Degaussing System: (pronounced de-gow-sing) electrical gear which sets up a neutralizing magnetic field to protect a ship from floating mines or torpedoes. It consisted of a huge cable that ran inside the hull and was energized to thwart mines and torpedoes. (Information courtesy www.USMM.org)

15. Trapezius muscle: A large diamond-shaped muscle that extends from the back of the skull to the lower part of the Thoracic spine(the part of the spine in the chest) and at its broadest point, across the width of the shoulders. The trapezius muscle helps support the neck and spine. Source: *The American Medical Association Home Medical Encyclopedia*

Made in the USA